# Developing Employee Capital

Setting the Stage for Lifelong Learning

David Kalamas

Joan Berry Kalamas

**HRD Press**, Inc.

Amherst, Massachusetts

Published by HRD Press, Inc.
22 Amherst Road
Amherst, Massachusetts 01002
1-800-822-2801 (U.S. and Canada)
1-413-253-3488
1-413-253-3490 (fax)
http://www.hrdpress.com

ISBN 0-87425-768-9
Printed in Canada

Typeset by Pracharak Technologies (P) Ltd., Madras, India
Cover design by Eileen Klockars
Editorial services by Suzanne Bay and Sally Farnham

# Contents

# CONTENTS

# List of Figures

# List of Tables

# Dedication

---

To my daughter, Jennifer Marie Kalamas, the light of my life—*David J. Kalamas*

To my father and mother, Duane and Betty Berry, who have provided me with love, support, guidance, and the belief that I could do anything I wanted to, and to Dr. Robert Berry, a truly terrific brother—*Joan Berry Kalamas*

# Introduction

Today's managers are starting to realize that developing their employees—their *human* resources—is critical to the success of their organization. If an organization is to remain viable in the long term, it must be able to continuously learn and adapt to constantly changing environments. The capability to learn and adapt to change rests not only on the shoulders of management, but on the shoulders of *all* employees. This book explains how managers can change the work environment to make it more conducive to employee development, and how they can help employees understand that *they are the organization*. The days of rewarding individual contributions will eventually come to an end: In the future, organizational success will be linked to team success. Individuals will have to learn on their own how to collaborate and develop themselves without a great deal of direction.

This book can help you redesign and rethink your strategies for the improvement of organizational functioning. It includes information on organization development and individual developmental strategies. It also includes reproducible assessment tools, lists of commercially available tools, process checklists, planning forms, ROI computation guides, a training decision matrix, basic job analysis forms, and step-by-step instructions for designing, implementing, and evaluating developmental strategies.

## Some Thoughts on How to Use This Book

This book has been designed to help you and your employees *jointly* create development plans. We recommend that you first review the developmental strategies described in Chapters 2 through 9, and then create *two* plans for each developmental effort: One plan to serve as a guide for your employee, and another plan to guide your own efforts. The employee's plan will be based on assessment data you collect, as well as on developmental goals and objectives you set together. Your plan will consist of the employee's plan and the actions *you* must take to set the developmental stage. (Worksheets that can be used to create these plans are provided throughout this book and in the appendix.) The complete developmental plan for a given employee, which will be built up over time, must be individualized. Assessment data must be kept private; many employees will not want to share personal feelings and desires with others— especially as they relate to the organization and fellow employees. Confidential files containing such information will be part of each person's individual plan. Adjustments can be made over time as conditions change.

# Chapter 1

# Laying the Foundation

## Why Help Employees Develop Themselves? A Closer Look

Renowned management authority Peter Drucker has contended for years that one of the primary tasks of any manager is to help his or her people develop themselves as employees and as individuals. Drucker holds that all development is self-development: Managers cannot direct people to develop themselves, but they can "set the stage."

In today's turbulent, rapidly changing business environment, companies can no longer rely solely on traditional venues for gaining a competitive edge. In the past, acquiring the newest technologies, continually doing a better job of managing financial resources, and marketing products or services more effectively than the competition allowed companies to gain an advantage in the marketplace. Today, the playing field has been leveled: Most companies have access to the same or similar technologies and can hire people with the necessary skill sets, leaving few with a significant edge. As D. Quinn Mills of the Harvard Business School notes, "The only sustainable advantage that any organization is going to have in the future is the ability of its people." The ability of companies to develop their human resources is and will continue to be key to organizational success.

To be successful, companies must create a climate that encourages employees to continuously develop themselves, become better performers in their own domains, and take ownership for the organization's success (or failure). Let's take a look at some of the potential benefits of setting the stage for employee development.

As we mentioned earlier, gaining a competitive edge in the marketplace is one major benefit, but there are others that should be considered in relation to the developmental puzzle. Some of these are summarized below:

- Employees who are skilled at the self-development process can help create a more flexible workforce that is better able to respond to changing market conditions.

- Independent learners and thinkers can more quickly refocus their thinking and direction.

- The more knowledgeable and skilled an employee is, the greater their capacity for self-monitoring—the ability to make mid-stream course corrections. The greater this capacity is the less likely the organization will face legal issues (discrimination claims, violation of governmental regulations, and so on).

- Employees who know that the organization is concerned about their development are less likely to willingly terminate their employment. Improvements in retention levels allow the organization to become more flexible and responsive to changing conditions and conserve organizational resources that might otherwise be expended replacing employees.

- Employees who work at self-development generally improve the organization's overall capabilities.

- Better training for employees helps provide a workforce better able to support the organization's mission and strategy.

- Employees who are more knowledgeable about the organization and their role in it as it relates to organizational success are likely to have more positive attitudes and increased loyalty to the organization.

- Employees who are allowed to cross-train become more valuable to themselves and to the organization.

It is important to remember that employee development (and organization development) is an ongoing, multilevel process. Development efforts must be ongoing, and they must be carried out in light of the interrelationships and interdependencies that exist in all organizations.

## Looking Ahead

In our view, any developmental effort must be based on a picture of what your organization will look like in the future—a vision. There are untold numbers of books, articles, white papers, and so on that support the need for a sound vision.

Most of the authors contend—and we agree—that a vision is an essential component of effective organizational leadership. A realistic picture of your organization and a realistic assessment of the forces that might affect your organization in the future are critical planning tools. Before you begin to plan for human resource development, be sure you have a good sense of your organization's strengths and weaknesses. You must also have an understanding of the potential opportunities that await you, as well as any potential threats to productivity and even organizational survival. A good starting point is to review your company's vision statement, mission statement, organizational goals, and organizational strategies (long-term, short-term, and operational). Solid data about where you are and where you want to be as a company will help you and your employees create more-effective developmental plans that integrate employee needs with organizational needs and improve the odds that your plans will contribute to maximized organizational functioning.

## The Nature of Organization Development

As the name implies, organization development (OD) is concerned with the development (improved functioning) of organizations. It is a branch of applied behavioral science based on the idea that the application of behavioral science techniques can help employees and organizations function at a higher and improved level. We will adopt the definition used by Michael Beer and Anna Louise Walton:

> Applying theory from psychology and organizational behavior, organization development (OD) comprises a set of actions undertaken to improve organizational effectiveness and employee well-being. These actions or "interventions" are typically designed and sequenced by an OD consultant following his/her diagnosis of an organization's needs and shortcomings. The tool kit these practitioners draw on ranges from organization-wide changes in structure to psychotherapeutic counseling sessions with groups and individuals.

We agree with most of the elements of this definition except the "OD consultant" element. It's true that many interventions are carried out by practitioners, but there are many that can and should be carried out by managers, albeit with occasional assistance. Such interventions include process improvement, redesign of work flow, changes to compensation and reward systems, employee training, employee development, establishment of missions and goals, structural redesign, physical environment redesign, and the purchase of appropriate technologies. In our view, there are many potentially positive interventions that can be initiated by managers.

OD is concerned with development of the organization as a whole, but as noted above, it is also concerned about the development of individual employees. After all, individual employee contributions determine the long-term success or failure of any and all organizations. We sometimes tend to overlook the fact that market position, financial support, and the latest technologies are all for naught if they cannot be supported by a highly skilled and experienced workforce. It goes without saying that all managers have a vested interest in and a duty to help develop their organizations.

## Learning Organizations

During the past few years, you have probably heard discussions about the "learning organization." Perhaps your own company is adopting practices, modifying strategies and structures, and creating or refining processes that will enable it to better initiate and/or respond to change—some of the key capabilities and features of learning organizations. Obviously change is the only constant in today's organizational environment. Effective response to change has become a very important capability for all organizations.

Change management has been the focus of a great deal of recent research. One of the most prominent researchers in this field is Peter Senge. In his book *The Fifth Discipline: The Art and Practice of the Learning Organization* (1990), he describes the features and characteristics that learning organizations must possess and the role of systems thinking in organizational success (his "fifth discipline"). In this book and in later publications, Senge laid out a path with guideposts rooted in part in General Systems Theory (GST)—a theory that strives to explain how all systems function (including organizational systems). GST is a tool that organizations can employ in their efforts to successfully manage change, thereby improving organizational performance. GST principles provide a way of viewing organizational systems as interrelated, interdependent parts that together determine long-term organizational success or failure.

As a manager, it is important that you see the whole "organizational picture" so that you can better determine the consequences of actions that modify system parts. Since employees are, in essence, system parts, it is imperative that you consider the ramifications of helping your employees acquire skills and knowledge, and modify their attitudes. As you and your employees create developmental plans, it will be beneficial if both of you maintain a "whole system" view of your organization.

As we mentioned above, there are characteristics and features that serve to define learning organizations, at least in part, since there is really no single set of descriptors that defines what is or isn't a learning organization. But there are a number of common features that should be considered if you are attempting to help your company become a learning organization (as you can see, that's where we're headed). Your company's chances for success improve if you create a learning organization environment, which will require the following components:

- A shared vision. You, all your employees, and the entire organization should share a picture of the future.

- Empowered employees. As much as possible, you should truly empower your employees. They should have the ability to make independent decisions and take action as needed. Be sure that they possess or can acquire the skills and knowledge to be successful.

- Strategy. Business strategy should emerge from the top *and* the bottom of the organization.

- Culture. A strong culture with shared values and beliefs helps lead to success in the marketplace.

- Information. The organization should be flooded with information and shared ideas.

- Boundaries. Do what you can to reduce or eliminate internal boundaries and roadblocks to effective communication.

## Performance Roadblocks

There are a number of roadblocks to job performance that you should be reminded of if you are to effectively aid your employees in their quest for self-development. Some of these roadblocks are listed below, along with actions you can take to eliminate or minimize their impact:

- Lack of motivation. Employee motivation can be supported by making sure that employees are involved in problem solutions and that they have concrete, achievable goals to work toward. People can become de-motivated if reward systems and performance consequences are inappropriate or nonexistent.

- Inadequate or inappropriate skills, knowledge, and attitudes. Formal training, guided practice, and feedback on performance can be valuable improvement strategies (more on this later).

5

♦ Job/organization mismatch. Be sure that employees are properly matched to their jobs and the organization, based on your determinations during the initial assessment.

♦ System obstacles. You might be able to remove obstacles based on your knowledge of organizational policies and procedures and come up with creative alternatives that your employees are unaware of.

♦ Inadequate resources. You might be able to help employees adjust their expectations or standards and aid in more efficient use of available resources.

♦ Ineffective communication. You and your employees can work together to define roles and responsibilities, and set priorities.

As we see it, the first step on the path to setting the stage is to first assess the overall situation in terms of employee needs and wants, and then balance them against the reality of organizational needs. (See Figure 1 for a graphic of the process.)

## The Developmental Assessment Process

Step 1—Gather employee data from employee and organizational records. (Human Resources department)

Step 2—Collect appraisal data and information from other managers. Examine performance records.

Step 3—From employee, gather information about his or her needs and wants.

Step 4—List current and future company needs in terms of positions and position requirements.

Step 5—Consider the impact of employee limitations and capabilities and available organizational resources (for training, compensation, and so on).

Step 6—Compare employee desires against organizational needs and resources.

Step 7—Prioritize needs, short- and long-term.

Step 8—With employee, create a development plan.

## Worksheets

As you begin this process, we recommend that you establish a file for *each* employee you will be working with on developmental planning. Since most of the data you collect is likely to be sensitive, it should be kept in a secure location. Worksheets that can be used by you and your employees follow.

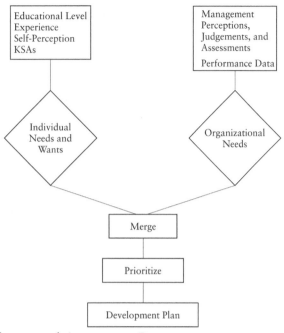

**Figure 1:** The Developmental Assessment Process

## Employee Self–Assessment 1

This assessment helps employees assess their capabilities and attitudes. The instrument addresses skills, knowledge, attitudes toward the company and toward one's job, basic career goals, and perceived need for additional education, training, or experience.

## Employee Data

This worksheet can be used to create a preliminary picture of the employee's levels of skill and knowledge and general performance.

## Projected Position Desires

The information collected for this worksheet provides an initial assessment of the positions for which an employee is currently suited or positions they are interested in.

## Employee Self-Assessment 1

Name _____     Date _____

**DIRECTIONS:** Answer the questions listed below. The answers to these questions will help you and your supervisor begin the process of creating a developmental action plan. PLEASE RESPOND HONESTLY.

1.  List the skills that you believe you possess.

_____

_____

_____

_____

_____

_____

2.  List areas that you know something about (business-related and non-business-related). Be creative.

_____

_____

_____

_____

_____

_____

3.  Rate how you feel about your current job.

☐ Don't like it much.     ☐ It's okay.     ☐ It's a great job.

4.  Rate how you feel about the company.

☐ Can't wait to quit.     ☐ I don't mind it.     ☐ I wouldn't work anywhere else.

5. On the scale below, rate your work environment by placing a ✓ at the appropriate spot.

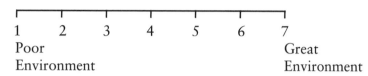

1    2    3    4    5    6    7
Poor                     Great
Environment        Environment

6. What job would you like to be doing . . . ?
Next year _____
Five years from now _____

7. What do you think you'll have to do to get there?
Education needs:

_____

_____

_____

_____

Training needs:

_____

_____

_____

_____

Experiences:

_____

_____

_____

_____

9

## Employee Data

(To be completed by the Manager)

Employee _____  Current position _____

Position date _____  Employment date _____

Completed by _____  Completion date _____

Education level _____

Time in present position (years/months) _____

Special skills:

_____
_____
_____
_____

Special knowledge:

_____
_____
_____
_____

Summary of most recent performance appraisal:

_____
_____
_____
_____
_____
_____

**10**

Information from other managers, the Human Resources department, and peers regarding job performance, relationship skills, motivators, perceived capabilities, and limitations:

_____

_____

_____

_____

_____

_____

_____

_____

_____

_____

_____

## Projected Position Desires

This listing relates to positions that the employee desires to hold in the future *and* for which he or she currently possesses the required knowledge and skills (or can acquire them prior to position availability).

| Projected Positions | | | Position Requirements |
|---|---|---|---|
| Position Title | Date Available | Number of Positions Open | |
| _____ | _____ | _____ | _____ |
| | | | _____ |
| | | | _____ |
| | | | _____ |
| | | | _____ |
| | | | _____ |
| | | | _____ |
| | | | _____ |
| | | | _____ |
| Position Title | Date Available | Number of Positions Open | |
| _____ | _____ | _____ | _____ |
| | | | _____ |
| | | | _____ |
| | | | _____ |
| | | | _____ |
| | | | _____ |
| | | | _____ |
| | | | _____ |
| | | | _____ |

| Projected Positions | | | Position Requirements |
|---|---|---|---|
| Position Title | Date Available | Number of Positions Open | |
| | | | |
| | | | |

## Assessment Tools

Since one of your goals is to help your employees develop themselves, we have included brief descriptions of assessment tools that your employees can use to obtain information about themselves. We have also included some additional tools and techniques that you can use to aid you in the planning process.

## Tools for Employees

Books

There are many excellent paper-based career-planning guides available commercially. Most of them are in workbook formats and include various instruments designed to allow the reader to assess their career goals, conduct career planning, and make an assessment of various personal characteristics such as personality, interests, abilities, and experiences.

Web Sites

The Web also provides a large number of very good resources for self-assessment. We've listed four of these below.

Helpful Web sites:

www.keirsey.com/contents.html.
This site allows people to complete the Keirsey Temperament Sorter (in any of seven different languages) without charge. Employees can use the results of this inventory to determine their Myers-Briggs personality type.

http://cbweb9p.collegeboard.org/career/html/searchQues.html.
This inventory, developed by the College Board, is a career questionnaire that assesses interests and abilities by asking questions that fall into various categories: temperament, abilities, working conditions, education, interests, and salary requirements. Responses are scored upon completion and a report is sent.

www.psychometrics.com/scales/tstart.html.
This site, copyrighted by Lionel Arsenaul and Psychometrics Canada Ltd., provides employees with an opportunity to complete the TRIMA Career Competency Questionnaire. The questionnaire consists of 150 questions and takes about 15 minutes to complete. As with most online assessments, responses are immediately scored and interpreted.

www.queendom.com/test frm.html.
This site provides numerous links to a variety of career/job assessments, including assessments that measure coping skills, time management, leadership, assertiveness, and personality type.

## Employee Assistance Programs (EAPs)

Many EAPs have been designed to deal primarily with employee health issues, but some provide career-counseling services. If you're unsure about the services your company provides, check with your HR department.

## Workshops and Seminars

There are many workshops and seminars available to the general public that deal with career-related issues (career decisions, time management, stress management, managing personal finances, retirement planning, and so on). Check industry publications for advertisements and contact professional organizations to which you belong. Your Human Resources department is also a good source of employee development–related information. Private consulting organizations can provide custom-designed programs for your company.

## Tools for Managers

### Workplace Observation

Valuable information can be acquired by observing what happens day-to-day in the workplace. Spend time unobtrusively observing to gather information related to concerns about the work environment, attitudes toward the organization, perceptions of fellow employees, and so on. This type of background data might help you when the time comes to create developmental action plans.

### Interviews

Consider conducting interviews with supervisors, work leaders, work teams, coordinators, individual job performers, and so on. We recommend that you prepare your questions ahead of time to minimize lost work time and prevent yourself from getting off-track. It's also a good idea to make sure that employees know why you are there and how it will benefit them.

## Developmental Strategies

The descriptions below provide rationales for employing the strategies described in detail in Chapters 2 through 9. This overview will serve as a helpful reference when you and your employees begin to create action plans and make a case for the expenditure of resources for employee development.

### Career Planning

Planning for career success is probably more important now than ever, since there are fewer options available within most organizations. Employees (and the organization) might have to be more creative when it comes to finding or providing opportunities for career advancement.

### Training

Given the speed at which many jobs are now evolving, it is incumbent upon employers to try to keep pace by providing several learning avenues. Formal training is one of an organization's most important development tools. By providing well-designed training programs, companies can keep job skills current.

Cross-training is likely to improve an employee's self-image, while at the same time increasing the ability of an organization to respond to changing demands. Retraining might open up new career paths.

## Mentoring

A skilled mentor can provide valuable direction to any employee, but especially a new one or one who is changing his or her career direction. The mentor understands the ins and outs of succeeding in the organization. By making use of their experience, employees can often avoid the same mistakes the mentor has made and become a more effective employee sooner.

## Coaching

An effective coach aids immeasurably in the self-development process. Guided feedback provided at the right time allows a job performer to make appropriate corrections to their performance on a timely basis.

## Job Enrichment and Enlargement

Individual responses to jobs vary. A job might be fascinating to one person, but not to someone else. Depending on how the job is designed, it can provide an opportunity for employees to satisfy their job-related needs. Redesign of jobs might pay substantial dividends in terms of satisfaction levels and retention.

## Educational Activities

These activities often help employees become better self-directed learners, since many educational programs assume that the participant will take what they have learned in a classroom or online and apply it in the workplace. Broader education also usually makes for better decision makers and problem solvers.

## Human Resource (HR) Planning

Some variation on succession planning might be called for as part of the general HR planning process. Although succession planning usually involves mid-level and upper-level managers, it is advisable (if resources are available) to move replacement planning to a lower level. At times, critical jobs and job functions exist at lower levels. For example, Information Technology positions are absolutely critical to most organizations, but they are very difficult and expensive to fill. It might be advisable to help someone develop the skills for such a position.

## Other Strategies

Training employees to be trainers of other employees is an excellent strategy. Acting as a trainer gives an employee a much better understanding of a topic area than through any other method because they must understand the topic thoroughly to be maximally effective at helping someone else learn it. Other strategies (task force membership, special projects, job rotation) provide sundry benefits to both the organization and the employee.

Now that you've acquired an understanding of the assessment process, you're ready to begin meeting with employees. Good luck!

# Chapter 2

# Career Planning

## The Nature of Careers

A career can be defined as *the sequence of work-related positions a person occupies throughout life*. A career plan, in our view, includes an assessment of employees' current career perspectives and future career goals, along with alternative paths for reaching those goals (developed in light of organizational constraints and individual characteristics and needs). In Chapter 1, we began to lay the assessment groundwork for an overall developmental plan. We see a career plan as part of this overall plan—an overall career "picture" that will help you and your employees make sound decisions about which developmental activities (training, acquiring a mentor or coach, redesigning jobs, and so on) will best meet their short- and long-term needs.

As we noted earlier, employees are less likely to leave the organization if they feel they are part of it and have a future within it. Increased retention levels provide many advantages, and they are just one of the many positive outcomes that will accrue if you and your employees invest the time and effort to create realistic career plans. To help you with your planning efforts, a number of assessment and planning tools are included at the end of this chapter.

Before we move on, it is important to note that the psychological contract between employees and their companies has changed in recent years. Historically, the unstated "contract" or understanding was that the company would provide continued employment and advancement opportunities if the employee remained with the company and performed his or her job at a high level. Organizational structures are "flatter," now. Work is organized on a customer or client basis, rather than on function, and many companies are downsizing. Authority has been pushed "down" and no longer rests exclusively at upper-management levels. Thus, instead of offering traditional job security, companies can help prepare employees to succeed with their current *and* future employers by providing developmental experiences that will help them cope with changing requirements.

## Competing Needs and Goals

In most organizations, competing needs and goals exist in many areas: staffing practices, retention strategies, restructuring, job design, downsizing strategies, and strategic plans. It is no different in the area of employee development: Individual employees, the organization itself, and managers all have different needs and goals in relation to employee development. Many employees are concerned about the reduced chances for upward mobility and the availability of lateral transfers. They also worry about the characteristics of specific jobs (the degree of task variety, meaningfulness, the task completion quotient, etc.); and whether or not the transfer will work with their own interests, values, and work preferences. Thus, employee needs and goals tend to focus more on individual issues. The organization (upper management) tends to view employee development on a more global scale—succession planning, replacement planning, employee possession of appropriate skill sets, cross-training strategies, and so on. The typical manager focuses on development issues that relate directly to the performance of his or her area of responsibility—employee motivation, improved retention, and skill improvement to enhance productivity. As you might guess, successful management of career development programs won't be possible unless you can strike a balance between these competing needs and goals. This relationship is illustrated in Figure 2.

## Career Stages

All "careers" are characterized by a move through four generally recognized stages: exploration, establishment, maintenance, and disengagement. We will examine each of these in turn.

- ♦ **Stage 1—Exploration.** This is the stage when individuals begin to think about identifying a type of work or occupation that interests them. In this stage (generally occuring from the teens to the early-to-late twenties),

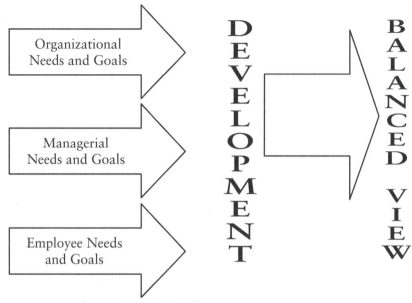

**Figure 2:** Competing Needs and Goals

21

people seek information at career fairs and from friends and relatives, co-workers, libraries, and the like. Exploration continues with the person's first job, as they evaluate additional career options. Until they gain adequate job experience, they usually require a good deal of direction and support to be successful. It's very important for the company at this point to provide orientation programs and well-thought-out socialization activities so that new employees can be assimilated into the organization's culture and become contributors as soon as possible.

◆ **Stage 2—Establishment.** In this stage, individuals find their place in the organization and begin to be independent contributors. Along with providing contributions to the success of the company, they begin to achieve financial stability and realize how their efforts and relative importance to organizational success are viewed by the company. This is the stage at which you and your employees will do most of their developmental planning.

◆ **Stage 3—Maintenance.** As the name implies, the employee in this stage is concerned with keeping his or her skills up-to-date and being perceived by appropriate people as a significant contributor to the company's success. Individuals in this stage are often sought after for advice and direction in terms of company policies, goals, and strategies due to their years of experience and knowledge of the company and their jobs. Mentors are usually drawn from this group.

◆ **Stage 4—Disengagement.** In this stage, individuals prepare to retire, reduce their work hours, or leave the company for various reasons—downsizing, a career change, or incompatibility with the work environment. Many employees are now opting for phased retirement when possible. This is often a win-win situation for both the company and the employee. The company gets to take advantage of the experienced employee's knowledge and skill and reduce the costs associated with hiring and training a new employee. When employees do leave the company, they often "recycle" back to the exploration stage that involves reevaluation and reexploration of skills, value systems, interests, and potential employment opportunities.

It's important to note that many companies are facing shortages of skilled employees in certain areas. To cope with these shortages, some companies retrain employees from other fields with the hope of recycling them into new jobs and careers. This type of strategy can help reduce replacement costs, since employees who are currently employed by the company already possess certain basic knowledge—of the company, of the industry, of competition, and so on. The implications for the company and the employees are obvious.

## Individual Issues

If you, as a manager, wish to change the way you manage people or interact with your employees on an interpersonal level, you must first understand yourself. You must make an effort to honestly assess your behavior patterns and determine why you behave as you do. To create a realistic and appropriate career plan, the same holds true—self-knowledge is critical. Honest assessment of your likes, dislikes, interests, values, and personal goals is a prerequisite for development of a viable career plan. In addition to personal characteristics that influence the nature of career plans, there are a number of organizational and societal issues that might also have an impact on planning. We've summarized some of these below.

### Career Plateaus

Members of the baby-boomer generation have already reached midlife, and many large employers are downsizing or flattening their organizational structures. As a consequence, increasing numbers of employees are finding themselves at career plateaus. If plateauing is a possibility in your organization, you and your employees might have to make preparatory adjustments by developing alternative plans. Unfortunately, these changes suggest that careers are going to be less predictable than in previous decades.

## Dual-Career Couples

As we are all well aware, many more women have joined the workforce in the past few decades, increasing the number of dual-career couples. It is important that you and your employees remain aware of issues that might affect career planning and progression. Periodic developmental reviews should touch on the issue. Some companies have reported successful resolution of career issues by involving the spouse in the process, even though they might not be employed by the company. This is not the norm, but there might be situations in which spousal involvement is appropriate. Issues often revolve around relocation (purchasing a new home, getting the children into a new school system, the quality of the local school system, availability of medical care, etc.). Check with your HR department to see what support services are available (payment of agency fees, reimbursement for job-seeking trips, local job bank access, and so on).

## Generational Differences

Different generations of employees are likely to have different career concerns based (at least in part) on differing value and belief systems. Generational differences do not always apply to all generation members, but there are a number of common traits that should be considered. One typology that is generally agreed upon contains the following generational groups: Milleniums or Generation Y'ers (in 2004, they are age 1–early 20s), Generation X'ers (in 2004, they are in their mid-20s to early 40s), Baby Boomers (in 2004, they are in their mid-40s to late 50s), and Traditionalists or Veterans (in 2004, they are in their late 50s to early 80s) so-called. Milleniums are often concerned about challenging work, global issues, and health issues. They tend to accept nontraditional family structures, change, and additional training in order to retain and enhance their employability. They usually have high expectations of the organization. Generation X'ers tend to be independent thinkers, entrepreneurial, team players, and flexible, and are comfortable with new technologies. On the down side, Gen X'ers tend to bring personal concerns into the workplace, don't want to hold people accountable, and have a hard time accepting authority. Baby Boomers tend to be idealistic and competitive, and question authority. Traditionalists tend to be patriotic, loyal, and fiscally conservative, and have faith in institutions. They are also concerned about having their experience valued, and have more respect for previous generations.

Psychological Issues

There are a number of internal issues that plague all of us and affect our work performance and interpersonal relationships. As a manager, it is part of your responsibility to point your employees in an appropriate direction for help with psychological issues should they affect work performance. Many organizations offer Employee Assistance Programs (EAPs) that provide confidential individual and family counseling. If your organization does not, direct employees to private or governmental sources. Talk with your HR department to get further information.

Increasing people's self-awareness and self-understanding is important if you are to truly help your employees create more-effective career and developmental plans. Work life and developmental efforts are affected if individuals feel that everyone else is more successful than they are, or if they experience burnout, a midlife crisis, a lack of motivation whose source cannot be readily identified, a lack of commitment and focus, or a fear of failure. Once again, it is not your responsibility to fix these problems, but you might be able to point your employees in the right direction.

## Facilitating the Exploration Process

Most of your employees will look to you for career advice as they explore options. You are viewed as a primary source of "inside" information that they know they need to succeed. In your management role of career guide, you are responsible for helping the employee meet personal needs as well as company needs. There are four generally accepted responsibility "hats" you wear as a manager: The first of these is *coach*. As a coach, you must listen to and define concerns, and assist in the career assessment process. As an *evaluator of performance,* the second role you play, you provide performance feedback and clarify company standards, job requirements, and company needs. As an *advisor,* you must help generate enriching work experiences, provide general direction on succeeding within the organization, and help with goal setting and action planning. As a *"linking pin,"* the fourth role, you link employees to career resources, but also help with networking within the organization to connect employees with possible sources of career help and information.

## A Process Model

There are many career development process models—useful tools that provide a conceptual framework for thinking about and comparing processes and concepts. Described below is a four-step process that should help you and your

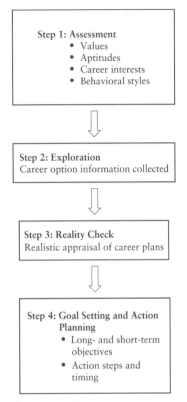

**Figure 3:** The Career Development Process

25

employees keep on track as you develop your career plans. A graphic of the process is provided in Figure 3.

Step 1—**Assessment**. Assessment, or self-assessment, refers to activities directed at acquiring personal information related to values, aptitudes, career interests, and behavioral tendencies (styles). Many psychological tests are designed to measure interest in certain occupations and jobs and the type of work environment an individual prefers. Some of these must be administered and scored by a psychologist or a credentialed administrator, but some can be self-administered or administered by a non-credentialed person. Some tests also measure the relative value an employee places on work and leisure activities. As we noted in Chapter 1, there are a number of Web sites that allow employees to complete various instruments for a minimal charge or at no charge (a number of colleges and universities sponsor some of these sites as career decision aids for prospective students). These instruments can help employees assess the current state of their career and plan for future career moves. There are also many paper-based instruments on the market (FIRO-B is a good example). Your HR department can help you and your employees determine the most appropriate instruments for the information you are seeking. Perhaps your organization provides career counseling services.

In addition to interests, behavioral styles (how we tend to interact with others), aptitudes for certain types of jobs, and values, we feel that an assessment must also include a look at career goals and priorities and potential environmental risks (within the organization). We have provided a number of self-assessment tools at the end of the chapter to aid you in this process.

Step 2—**Exploration.** This stage involves collection and examination of career option information. We see the manager's roles in this stage as those of *linking pin* and *advisor* (as noted above). Employees are sometimes unaware of career information sources and activities. Your company might sponsor career workshops that deal with goal setting, self-assessment, networking, and so on. There might be job postings on bulletin boards or company Web sites. HR might provide career planning workbooks, career counseling services, and career path information. If your employees are interested in certain jobs, you might be able to set up meetings with people currently in those positions and create access that your employees cannot accomplish on their own. The key to this stage lies in helping your employees collect data that will allow them to make sound career decisions.

Step 3—**Reality Check.** This stage is the point where you and an individual employee take a realistic look at the positive and negative circumstances related to career planning. Questions to ask: Where does the employee fit into company plans? What promotion possibilities exist? What about lateral transfers? Are the employee's career goals realistic? Do organizational constraints exist? Is there a real possibility of relocation? Will the employee relocate? Is the employee flexible and ready for new opportunities? These checking questions and others that you feel are pertinent should be addressed periodically during the planning process.

Step 4—**Goal Setting and Action Planning.** This final step allows you and your employees to state realistic long- and short-term career objectives that include potential resources and potential roadblocks. You will also establish timelines for action steps and set completion dates. You might also wish to establish sub-goals.

## Assessment and Planning Forms

The remainder of this chapter provides assessment and planning forms that will aid you and your employees in the development of a viable career plan: a work-value assessment, a career-priority assessment, a career risk assessment, a career goal-planning tool, a constraint analysis tool, and a comprehensive career planning document. The information you have derived from the assessment process described in Chapter 1, combined with the information derived from the forms and planning documents provided in this chapter, should allow you to create a sound career plan that will be a significant piece of the overall development plan.

### Employee Self-Assessment 2: Values

Values represent relatively stable basic convictions that there are preferable ways to act and be at individual and societal levels. Values begin to develop in childhood, when we are told that there are certain ways to behave or not to behave. As children, it is a "black-or-white" world. Values can be modified later in life if we decide that our underlying convictions that support the value no longer hold.

All values have a content attribute and an intensity attribute. The *content attribute* states that a certain way of being or behaving is important, while the *intensity attribute* specifies how important it is. If we rank our values in terms of their relative intensity or importance to us, we have defined our own value system. Values are important in organizational settings in that they lay the groundwork for attitudes and motivation, which partly determines how we behave in a given organizational setting. We enter organizations with preconceived notions of how things "ought to be." If our perceptions are inaccurate, we are likely to be disappointed. It's our feeling that if you are creating a career or developmental plan, it is important that employees understand their own values, especially in relation to organizational values (which are part of the organizational culture). In order to achieve a good organizational "fit," there should be significant overlap between employee values and organizational values. Self-Assessment 2 is included in the book because we believe that it helps individuals identify what is most important to them.

## Employee Self-Assessment 3: Career Priorities

As we know, values are relatively stable. Needs, on the other hand, will change as our circumstances change. A powerful need at one point in time can become a less-powerful driving force after that need is met or our circumstances change. For example, salary might be very important when we are beginning our career, putting children through college, and so on. It might be considerably less important later on, when our children have finished school and the house is paid for. It follows, then, that at different points in our careers, our needs and priorities differ. Self-Assessment 3 is a tool to rank-order current career priorities, providing a sense of what work-related considerations are most and least important at this point in time.

## Employee Self-Assessment 4: Career Risks

Risks abound in most organizations. If you and your employees are cognizant of risks to your careers, you'll be better able to make adjustments when events occur that can have an impact on your plans. Layoffs, burnout, and personality conflicts between team members, superiors, and peers can occur without much warning. If you've made a realistic assessment of the risks, you'll be better equipped to deal with events if and as they occur. Assessment 4 also addresses factors common to many strategic planning activities—SWOTs (strengths, weaknesses, opportunities, and threats). In our view, a successful career plan must contain a strategy element that allows you to first identify these issues and then develop ways to address them—play to your strengths, eliminate or minimize the impact of weaknesses, seize opportunities, and reduce or eliminate threats.

## Employee Self-Assessment 5: Career Goals

Career goals share the same features with other work goals. They should be specific, clearly stated, realistic, and understood by everyone, and they need to have a time element attached. Self-Assessment 5 helps employees think about their career goals and put them on paper, which increases the likelihood that goals will be reached. Although Assessment 5 is a self-assessment, it might be helpful if you sit down with your employees and review their goals in terms of the factors noted above. You might also wish to discuss types of goals—increased responsibility/promotion to a specific job, specific lifestyle changes, specific lateral transfers, skill-building (capability enhancement), and so on.

Employee Self-Assessment 6 : Force Field Analysis

Force field analysis is a technique used to identify the forces at work in a problem or goal environment that either restrain change or support change. At any given point in time, these forces are generally in balance and the status-quo is maintained. After you have identified these forces, you can take steps to increase the number or strength of supporting forces and eliminate or reduce the strength of restraining forces. Restraining forces might be things like lack of skills, lack of goal information, lack of experience, lack of visibility with key decision makers, and so on. Supporting forces might include timing, organizational staffing needs, the right skills, the right experience, and so on. Self-Assessment 6 can help you list restraining and supporting forces so that you can create a viable career plan.

29

## Employee Self-Assessment 2
## Values

Name _____  Date _____

To get a sense of your own value system, place a ✓ on the appropriate place on the scale to the right of the value. Trust your instincts, and don't spend too much time thinking about your values—your results will be more accurate if you respond quickly.

| VALUE | Always Valued | Often Valued | Sometimes Valued | Seldom Valued | Never Valued |
|---|---|---|---|---|---|
| Advancement | | | | | |
| Authority/Power | | | | | |
| Challenge | | | | | |
| Change and Variety | | | | | |
| Community | | | | | |
| Competence | | | | | |
| Competition | | | | | |
| Creativity | | | | | |
| Decision Making | | | | | |
| Family | | | | | |
| Group Affiliations | | | | | |
| Freedom/Independence | | | | | |
| Friendships | | | | | |
| Helping Others | | | | | |

| VALUE | Always Valued | Often Valued | Sometimes Valued | Seldom Valued | Never Valued |
|---|---|---|---|---|---|
| Influencing People | | | | | |
| Job Security | | | | | |
| Knowledge | | | | | |
| Moral Standards | | | | | |
| Personal Security | | | | | |
| Public Contact | | | | | |
| Recognition | | | | | |
| Religious Beliefs | | | | | |
| Salary Level | | | | | |
| Stability | | | | | |
| Status | | | | | |
| Supervision | | | | | |
| Working Alone | | | | | |
| Working under Pressure | | | | | |
| Working with People | | | | | |

# Employee Self-Assessment 3
## Career Priorities

Name _____   Date _____

Rank the items in the list below, using the scale of 1 to 10 (1 is the most-important consideration, and 10 is the least-important consideration at this time.) Remember, you can have only one number 1.

**Salary**
_____ (what you now earn)

**Potential**
_____ (Your probability for advancement or increase in earnings)

**Hours**
_____ (Scheduled number of hours you work)

**Kinds of Tasks**
_____ (Doing what you like to do; task variety; using your skills)

**Working Conditions**
_____ (Work setting, facilities, your work environment)

**Interpersonal Relations**
_____ (The quality of your interactions with your superior, co-workers, subordinates)

**Degree of Responsibility**
_____ (Level of decision making; amount of supervision you receive and give to others)

**Benefits**
_____ (Your benefits package)

**Location**
_____ (Location, including distance from your home to the job)

**Flexibility**
_____ (The flexibility you have in setting your own job hours and job tasks)

# Employee Self-Assessment 4
## Career Risks

Name _____ Date _____

1. Check the areas below for which you could be at risk within the next 12 months. By assessing your career risks, you will be better able to face change.

   _____ Layoffs
   _____ Rumored layoffs
   _____ Some of your skills will become obsolete
   _____ Personality conflicts with superiors, subordinates, or peers
   _____ Conflict between your values and those of the organization
   _____ Your age (being perceived as too young, too old, or having been with the organization too long)
   _____ Health risks
   _____ Unmanaged stress/burnout

2. Check the statements that best describe your career and work life.

   _____ My current job consumes and dominates my life. I often feel overwhelmed. I need to find time to build my career potential.
   _____ I have an alternate source of income that I can fall back on if my current career becomes untenable.
   _____ I can find fulfillment by doing volunteer work.
   _____ I regularly engage in self-development activities through training, self-directed study, and continuing education.
   _____ I possess skills, knowledge, and abilities that I don't use in my current career.

3. To assess your career strategic assets (which at times can be employed to minimize or eliminate career risks), describe the following:

   My career strengths:

   _____

   _____

   _____

   _____

33

My career weaknesses:

_____

_____

_____

_____

_____

_____

My career opportunities:

_____

_____

_____

_____

_____

_____

My career threats:

_____

_____

_____

_____

_____

_____

# Employee Self-Assessment 5
## Career Goals

Name _____     Date _____

A. Think about your future work life. In the space below, list all the goals you would like to achieve in the next 20 years. Try not to list your goals in general terms ("*I want to be successful*"). Instead, state your goals in specific terms ("*I want to complete my master's degree in Business Administration within the next five years*").

_____

_____

_____

_____

_____

_____

_____

_____

_____

_____

_____

_____

_____

B. Now, go back through your list of long-range goals. Place each goal that you've listed into one of the specific time frames listed below.

*Goals that you wish to achieve in the next 10 to 20 years:*

_____

_____

_____

_____

_____

*Goals that you wish to achieve in the next 5 to 10 years:*

_____

_____

_____

_____

_____

*Goals that you wish to achieve in the next 2 to 5 years:*

_____

_____

_____

_____

_____

*Goals that you wish to achieve within the next year:*

_____

_____

_____

_____

_____

C. Come back to this list in a few days, after you have had time to think about other goals you might have. Add these goals to your initial list. Your objective is to make it as complete as possible. Change or delete any goals that no longer seem appropriate. Remember that goals are not carved in stone—they might change as conditions change.

# Employee Self-Assessment 6
## Force Field Analysis

Name _____        Date _____

Restraining Forces                    Supporting Forces

## The Final Plan

The next two pages contain a document that can be used to create a complete career goal plan. The document is designed to allow creation of a plan for only one goal, so you'll want to make photocopies of the form prior to filling it out. A primary goal might be *To be promoted to section manager by the end of the calendar year.*

The enabling goals are sub-goals that must be reached before the primary goal stated at the beginning of the document is reached. There is space for four enabling goals, although there might be fewer for a given goal. An enabling goal might be *Get on-the-job training as an assistant section manager.* The action steps refer to activities that must be undertaken to reach an enabling goal. For example, *Attend the Section Manager Training course to prepare myself to work as an assistant section manager.* The remainder of the document provides space for you to think about and list sources of support, the resources you will need (and how you'll acquire them), and measurement criteria that will indicate when you have achieved your goals.

## **Career Goal Planning: The Final Plan**

Name _____     Date completed _____

GOAL

_____

_____

Barriers or roadblocks that might prevent me from reaching my goal:

_____

_____

_____

_____

Enabling Goal: _____

| Action Steps | Target date | Completed |
|---|---|---|
| _____ | _____ | ❑ |
| _____ | _____ | ❑ |
| _____ | _____ | ❑ |

Enabling Goal: _____

| Action Steps | Target date | Completed |
|---|---|---|
| _____ | _____ | ❑ |
| _____ | _____ | ❑ |
| _____ | _____ | ❑ |

**39**

Enabling Goal: _____

| Action Steps | Target date | Completed |
|---|---|---|
| _____ | _____ | ❑ |
| _____ | _____ | ❑ |
| _____ | _____ | ❑ |

Enabling Goal: _____

| Action Steps | Target date | Completed |
|---|---|---|
| _____ | _____ | ❑ |
| _____ | _____ | ❑ |
| _____ | _____ | ❑ |

**Support**

To achieve this goal, I should share it with:

_____

_____

_____

**Resources**

Resources I need to achieve this goal are:

_____

_____

_____

**Success Indicators**

I will know I have reached my goal when:

_____

_____

_____

# Chapter 3

# Training as a Developmental Tool

A number of considerations need to be made when you begin to plan training activities for your employees. First, identify the purpose of the training. In most situations, training activities should not be completed unless they ultimately contribute to improved organizational performance. This means you and your employees must understand where your organization is headed. You should review your company's strategic plan(s), mission statement, vision statement, and any operational goals/objectives that might be pertinent to your area. Appropriate training will help your employees grow and develop while helping your organization gain a competitive advantage in its markets. By helping your employees acquire the knowledge and skill they need to be successful, everyone wins. We'll address other considerations as we examine various aspects of employee training.

## The Nature of Training

Training refers to the activities undertaken to facilitate employee acquisition of the knowledge, skills, attitudes (KSAs) and behaviors that are critical for successful job performance. The ultimate goal is for employees to take these newly acquired or improved KSAs and behaviors and apply them to job tasks. This process is generally termed *transfer* of training. Although most training in the United States is now focused on basic technical skills and mid-management training, this situation will probably change in the coming years as our economy continues to move from a machine-based one to a knowledge-based one.

Therefore, intellectual capital (what people know and can do) will become increasingly critical to organizational success, requiring employees to acquire increasingly advanced knowledge and skills.

## How Learning Occurs

There are various definitions of the word *learning*, but the following definition is generally accepted.

> *Learning is a relatively permanent change in behavior that is the result of some experience.*

It follows, then, that to determine whether or not learning has occurred, one has to observe some behavioral change. For example, taking a written test after completing a course would indicate whether or not and to what degree a participant learned the material taught in the course. As an evaluator, you might also observe employees after they have returned to their work site. You could attempt to determine whether transfer and learning have occurred by watching for new behaviors that employees should have acquired as a result of participating in a course.

Learning job tasks, either by a new employee or by one who has more experience, generally follows a common sequence, as depicted in Figure 4. The first stage in this process is Unconcious Incompetence. When a person is in this stage, they are, at least to some degree, unaware of what they don't know, because they lack experience or job-related knowledge, or both. The second stage is Concious Incompetence. At this stage, the employee is aware of what they don't know and can't do. The third stage is Concious Competence. When employees are in this stage, they are aware *and* they have acquired sufficient skills and knowledge to adequately perform a given job task, but it takes a certain amount of concious thought for them to perform. When they reach the Unconcious Competence stage, they can perform at an adequate level without much concious thought. Continued practice after this point results in ever-increasing task performance speed and consistency.

In terms of *what* is learned, Gagne and Medsker in *The Conditions of Learning* (1996) offer a classification of learning outcomes that provides a basis for determining what capabilities should be acquired as a result of training. The classification also provides a tool that can be used by whoever is designing instruction. This classification is described below:

- ◆ **Verbal information.** This includes labels, facts, and various types of job knowledge. For example, a machine operator of a hydraulic-powered machine must know the names of various parts of the equipment *and* something about the science of hydraulics.

42

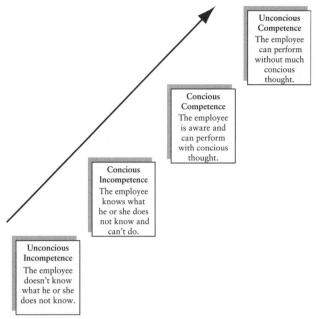

**Figure 4:** The Stages of Learning

- ◆ **Intellectual skills.** These include conceptual understanding and an understanding of what are termed *rules*, which are essentially tested and accepted ways of thinking about problems ("problems" here is defined very broadly). For example, in order for an employee to design a computer program, he or she must understand many computer-related concepts and the design process that must be employed (the "rules").

- ◆ **Motor skills.** These include gross- and fine-motor control of our physical movements. For example, a manufacturing plant maintenance person must be able to climb ladders and replace fluorescent light bulbs.

- ◆ **Attitudes.** Attitudes predispose employees to consistently behave in either a negative or a positive way to something, based on their unique beliefs. For example, if an employee has a positive attitude toward her work, you would expect her to exhibit behaviors that would indicate her attitude—doing her best work, helping other employees, trying to solve problems on her own, etc.

- ◆ **Cognitive strategies.** These mental strategies essentially control the *processes* of learning. How we address problems, how we make decisions, how we remember, and so on are controlled and directed by our cognitive or thinking strategies. These are partially determined by knowledge and experience levels. For example, a machine repairperson might address a troubleshooting issue with a variety of different mental strategies designed to solve a given machine operation problem. An experienced or expert troubleshooter will likely have more strategies at his or her disposal than a novice troubleshooter.

So far, we have examined the nature of training, a learning process, and what employees need to learn about types or categories of learning outcomes. To continue laying the groundwork for the development of individual training plans, we should consider how we might differentiate between training needs based on KSA deficiencies and systemic issues, both of which influence job performance.

## Identifying Nontraining Problems

If you and your employees are to create the most efficient training plan possible, it is critical that you conduct a root-cause performance analysis for each employee. In our experience, managers too often use training as a quick fix for performance problems. You've undoubtedly heard the old adage, "We've got a training problem." You might have one, or you might not. If you don't and you try a training fix, the consequences are obvious—resources are expended unnecessarily, the problem persists, and your employees' energies are diverted from the self-development path. About 30 years ago, Robert Mager and Peter Pipe wrote a book entitled *Analyzing Performance Problems* (1970). This groundbreaking work provided a very clear and insightful look at the most common situations in which poor or insufficient training is *not* the root cause. We've summarized these for you below:

- The performance discrepancy isn't important. If what the employee is doing (or not doing) doesn't really affect the company's overall performance goals (i.e., the bottom line), then there is really no basis for taking action. Remember our rationale for conducting training?
- The desired performance is punishing. Some things that an employee is requested to do produce what are perceived to be negative consequences, with no up side (for example, uprooting the employee's family and moving them across the country, just so the employee can fill a lesser position in the organization).
- Nonperformance is rewarded. Sometimes poorly designed reward systems provide positive reinforcement of various types to employees for *not* doing job tasks. The up side associated with nonperformance is greater than that associated with performance. For example, an employee might feel that a

very difficult task is not worth doing if they are not punished (or only mildly reprimanded) or not sufficiently rewarded. Not doing the task is perceived as its own reward.

♦ Performance doesn't matter to the employee. When performance of a job task is not periodically reinforced, then that performance will tend to disappear. In the same vein, if nonperformance is not punished, it will tend to continue.

♦ There are obstacles to performance. There are often obstacles to performance that are built into organizational systems. You've undoubtedly experienced many of them yourself: poor communication; conflicting demands; poor, antiquated, or inappropriate equipment; out-dated policies, procedures, and practices; role conflict; and unrealistic goals.

♦ The employee lacks practice. Sometimes employees just don't apply their skills often enough to maintain them at a high level.

♦ The employee lacks feedback. Without corrective feedback, employees often have no way of knowing whether they are on track or not. Feedback is critical to effective and improved performance.

♦ The job is too complicated. Some jobs were either designed poorly from the start or job evolution has created a job that the average performer cannot complete, even if they have the requisite knowledge and skills.

♦ The task is beyond the employee's physical or mental abilities. Employees might not have the inherent ability, might be overqualified, might be totally disinterested, etc. Whatever the reason for the mismatch, training will never solve this performance problem. The harsh reality is that transfer or termination might be the only solutions.

Figure 5 provides a graphic summary of the relationships between training and nontraining solutions to performance discrepancies or gaps that will be useful to keep in mind as you develop training plans. Please remember: Any training that is provided should have a *clearly defined purpose*.

45

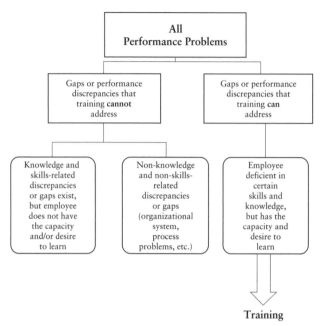

**Figure 5:** Training and Nontraining Solutions to Performance Problems

## Gap Analysis

Now that we have reaffirmed the idea that there are some performance problems that can be addressed by training and some that can't, we can look at a method for further defining problems in terms of potential causes and potential solutions. The model in Figure 6 illustrates a method for diagnosing discrepancies or **gaps** between employees' current capabilities and future/desired capabilities. It's important to note that by defining these gaps, you are both defining performance problems and setting training goals, which you can use to jointly develop training plans. The method for conducting a gap analysis is described below:

Step 1—**Assess the current capabilities of employees.** Make a list of the skills and knowledge your employees possess in relation to their current jobs. You can use employee self-reports and your own observations.

Step 2—**Determine desired (future) capabilities.** Make a list of the skills and knowledge your employees now possess that they feel might apply to other jobs they desire to hold in the future. Jointly list skills and knowledge that you or the employee feel they will need to acquire.

Step 3—**Consider how organizational realities might influence your training plans.** Organizational mission, strategies, goals, and resources might affect the design of your training plan. Make a list.

Step 4—**Consider how work design, job designs, and organizational factors might be influencing employee performance.** Remember, there are many factors that might influence performance, either negatively or positively.

Step 5—**Define the gap.** Based on the difference between what employees know and can do now and what they wish to know and to be able to do in the future and what the organization might require, you can define the gap in preparation for creating your training plans.

Step 6—**Determine possible causes for the gap.** There are many possible causes for a gap. Make a list. Refer to Figure 6 and/or refer to your own experiences. Getting input from other managers and your Human Resources department might facilitate this process.

Step 7—**Determine possible solutions to reduce or close the gap.** Make a list of possible activities and strategies aimed at closing or reducing the gap. Use the list provided in Figure 6 and/or refer to your own experiences. Copy this list for other managers and Human Resources.

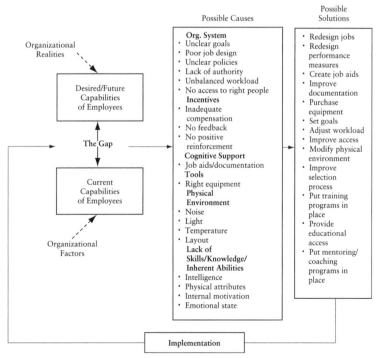

**Figure 6:** Gap Analysis

47

## What to Look For

Training programs should be designed to maximize the chances that participants will learn content (acquire skills and knowledge) that they will take back and use in their work environment to better perform job tasks (training transfer). When you and your employees begin to consider training programs and training providers (or sources), there are a number of program characteristics and features that you should look for that will indicate a sound program design. You can usually obtain copies of program materials or samples from vendors, from your training department, from publishers of materials, and through your Human Resources department. If a vendor is conducting training for another client, you might be able to join a class and observe their facilitator in action. It is especially helpful if you can obtain copies (or at least partial copies) of participant manuals and instructor/facilitator guides. If you are considering computer-based programs, many of the same instructional design principles apply. You might also wish to speak with others who might have used the same materials or attended the same programs you are considering. Most reputable vendors will provide you with client lists and past participant lists.

Training can be quite expensive when you consider the many and varied direct program costs, facilitator costs, lost production time, and occasional employee travel costs. If you are going to expend substantial resources, you should obtain the best return possible on your investment. You can help ensure this outcome if you take care in choosing training activities. It is not as difficult as it might appear to choose sound programs. The list below will help:

- ◆ **Training objectives.** Well-stated objectives are a *very* important part of any instructional program, since they determine program content and what will be evaluated at the end of the training program. They state what it is that participants will learn and how well they will learn it—they define the learning outcomes of the program. Each objective should specify the action that should be taken, the conditions under which the action should be performed, and the criteria or standards that the performer must meet so that the objective is accomplished successfully. They should look like this:

  *Given the technician's maintenance and installation guides (CONDITIONS), repair the telecommunications equipment (PERFORMANCE) according to the manufacturer's specifications (CRITERIA/STANDARDS).*

- ◆ **Learning goals.** Participants should be made aware of *why* they are attending training. Stating learning goals in language that employees understand and helping them see its value increases the chances that learning will occur.

◆ **Rehearsal/Practice.** Programs should contain multiple opportunities for practice and rehearsal. Role plays, simulations, and skill practices (with feedback) all contribute to effective learning. Repetition is the key.

◆ **Allowance for different learning styles.** Different people have different learning preferences. Some are visual learners, some are auditory learners, and some learn best by "getting their hands dirty" (kinesthetic learners). Well-designed programs allow for these different learning preferences (skill practices, videos, audiotapes, discussion opportunities, and graphics all contribute). The key is to have a variety of delivery modes.

◆ **Feedback opportunities.** As you know, feedback is critical if you wish to modify performance. Participants should receive feedback from the facilitator and peers (if appropriate).

◆ **Transfer mechanisms.** The closer the training environment is to the actual work environment of participants, the greater the likelihood of transfer—application of newly acquired skills in the work environment. It is also important that the environment employees return to after the program is a supportive one—employees must be able to practice what they have learned. Their supervisor or manager should understand the objectives of the training program and provide practice time and positive reinforcement when the employee returns to work. Many of the better programs also provide follow-up sessions after the program to further reinforce learning.

◆ **Evaluation.** There are four commonly accepted strategies for evaluating training programs. Program design should provide for one or more types to occur: reaction, learning, behavior, and results. We'll examine each of these later in the chapter when we discuss ROI for training.

## Adults as Learners

Since many of the developmental issues we are examining involve adults as learners, we felt it would be appropriate to mention some generally accepted assumptions regarding adult learners. These are noted below:

1. Adults generally want to know *why* they are learning something. Remember instructional goals?

2. Adults want to be *self-directed*. They want to set or help set their own learning path.

3. Adults enter learning situations with "baggage" and lots of work-related *experiences*. This provides a fertile ground for program discussion activities.

4. Adult motivation is usually both *intrinsic* (internal—for example, the desire to achieve) and *extrinsic* (provided from outside the performer—for example, money). At times either one or both types serve as learning motivators.

5. Adults enter most learning situations in a *problem-centered* mode. They often have work-related problems that they hope training will help them solve.

## Where to Look for Training Opportunities

There are a number of places that you and your employees can look for training opportunities. Keep in mind that quality and cost can vary considerably. We've listed the most commonly used sources below:

- **Internal training departments.** Your company's training department is most likely the best place to start. Take your training manager to lunch. Arrive armed with a list of training goals and needs for your employees that you can refer to if the opportunity presents itself. It is important to establish relationships with the staffs of your training and development or organizational development departments—the road will be smoother if you have established relationships with appropriate support staff. This relationship building is especially critical in today's business environment, since resources that can be devoted to training are often in short supply.

  Your training department can potentially support you in a number of ways. Staff members can develop and/or deliver job-specific programs (either internally or by outsourcing). They may be able to purchase or provide generic, off-the-shelf programs for you, they can provide advice on program purchases, they can help with implementation and evaluation plans, they can provide advice on developmental strategies, and they can provide insights on dealing with vendors (both out-of-towners and locals). They may also help prepare some of your own employees to be trainers. It is important to note that many programs can be delivered in different ways—in a self-study paper-based format, instructor-led (classroom) format, or computer-based format.

- **Vendors.** There are many vendors that can meet your training needs. Most specialize in a few areas, but there are many generalists as well. They can be located by visiting the Web, by contacting local or national training/OD organizations, or by means of referral from other organizations that might have employed their services. Some are listed in the local Yellow Pages. On the Web, simply enter "training" as a key word to your search engine, and you'll get a large number of vendor hits. Many vendors also have their own Web sites. You can visit the sites of the largest training/OD organizations and request catalogs or listings of vendors. You might want to visit the sites of: *The American Society for Training and Development (ASTD), The Society for Human Resource Management (SHRM),* and *The International Society for Performance Improvement (ISPI).* These national sites also have hyperlinks that can direct you to local chapters of their organizations. By means of a search engine, you can narrow your search by training topic (e.g., general technical, electronic repair training, software training, supervisory training, industrial training, customer service training, programmable controller training, etc.). Your Human Resource department or training department can also provide direction. A great deal of training is now available via the Internet and the Web. A word of caution, however: Quality and cost can vary considerably from vendor to vendor, and it is more difficult in many cases to make informed decisions about these products. You or your employees will probably want to try out these products before purchasing them. Most vendors will send you sample programs on request.

- ◆ **Educational institutions.** Many educational institutions provide training and development services in addition to their regular educational offerings. Some are subsidized by the federal government and state/local governmental entities. These subsidies often result in lower costs for clients. You may wish to contact local four-and two-year colleges, universities, and vocational schools. In our experience, these providers generally do a commendable job.

- ◆ **Self-study courses.** There are still many types of paper-based self-study materials available today. Professional organizations often produce or subsidize training materials for their own members. Many publishers provide self-study materials on almost every topic imaginable. Trade magazines, business publications, advertising materials, and the Web are often fruitful places to seek materials. Once again, your training or HR department can provide you with useful information.

- ◆ **E-learning (online learning).** E-learning refers to instruction and delivery of training by computer online through the Internet and Web. One major benefit of e-learning is that it goes beyond traditional learning to include delivery of information and tools that can improve performance (for example, Intelligent Tutoring Systems—ITSs). E-learning includes Web-based training, virtual classrooms, and distance learning.

Training programs on CD-ROMS or servers can be delivered through the Internet or through a company's own intranet, and displayed on a Web browser. E-learning can also be a source of task-based support and simulation-based training. Space does not permit a full treatment here, so if your organization has e-learning capabilities, we would certainly recommend further investigation.

Table 1 provides a list of Internet sites that describe many different types of resources available for employee training and development.

## Table 1: Training Resources

| Description of Site | Web Address |
|---|---|
| Home page for American Society for Training and Development (ASTD), access to Training and Development journal | www.astd.org |
| Access to training resources, training, training information, communications, and networking | www.trainingsupersite.com |
| Home page for Society for Human Resource Management (SHRM) | www.shrm.org |
| Reviews of media-based training products for business | www.tmreview.com |
| Home page for Center for Creative Leadership—management/leadership training, assessment, executive development | www.ccl.org |
| Site with information on training, Web-based training | www.multimediatraining.com/ |
| Home page for International Society for Performance Improvement (ISPI) performance-based instruction | www.ispi.org |
| Information on Web-based training | www.brandon-hall.com |
| Information on Electronic Performance Support Systems (EPSSs) | www.epsdsinfosite.com |
| Business simulation example | www.riskybusiness.com |
| Sample Web sites, tips for building Web sites | www.webbasedtraining.com |
| Online learning company | www.knowledgeplanet.com |

## Measuring Returns on Your Training Investment

When you arrange for someone to provide classroom training for your employees or choose some other delivery mode (computer-based training, for example), be aware of how learning outcomes are going to be measured. Without some measure of outcomes, you really have no way of knowing if employees have learned and how well they have learned. In addition, it is difficult to determine benefits of training, and to later support expenditures of training funds. It is also valuable to know what employees thought about their training experiences.

There are many training program evaluation models in use. One of the most popular is Donald Kirkpatrick's four-level evaluation model. It is widely used to evaluate training efforts, and holds great logical appeal. His model addresses four of the most important evaluation areas that are of interest to trainers. We've summarized these below:

**Level 1: Reaction.** Reaction can best be defined as how well participants liked a particular program. It could be described as an affective, subjective measure—measuring participants' *feelings* about the perceived quality of the program, the skills of the facilitator, whether or not the learning objectives were achieved, and so on. But it is *not* a measure of whether or not learning has occurred. Reaction, however, is easy to measure, and nearly all trainers do it.

**Level 2: Learning.** Measurement of learning is a more objective assessment of program outcomes, since participants are given a test of some sort after the program ends. Level 2 provides an assessment of what principles, facts, concepts, etc., were *assimilated* by participants. The best approach is to do a pretest before the learning and a posttest after so that you can get a sense of learning that occurred as a result of the program.

The best data is obtained if you are able to draw two random samples from the training population. One randomly selected group receives the training (the experimental group), and the other randomly selected group does not attend the training. Test results are then compared to determine if the program might have had an effect on learning. If the training target group is not large enough or if it is politically unfeasible, you might only be able to test the training group. It is very important to remember that *any* test must be linked to the program's stated learning objectives and course content. As a rule, test results based on training should *not* be used for human resource actions (promotion, pay increases, etc.).

**Level 3: Behavior.** Evaluation of behavioral change in the work environment is more difficult than measuring reaction and learning, but it is doable with the expenditure of a little more time and effort. Level 3 evaluation usually relies on the behavioral appraisals of the trainees themselves (self-reports), and their supervisors, peers, and others familiar with the trainees' on-the-job behaviors. Again, a before-and-after approach is called for. The best-designed programs also call for follow-up appraisals a few months after the program to determine if the newly learned behaviors have "stuck."

**Level 4: Results.** Results are measured to determine the payoff to the company from a training program. Payoffs are usually stated in terms of desired results such as reduced costs, reduced turnover, higher quality, fewer accidents, and increased production. As you might imagine, measurement of results is more difficult due to potential intervening variables, but it is possible in some situations and is very desirable. Level 4 data is powerful: You (the evaluator) can really say something about the quality and effectiveness of a given training program.

**Return on Investment (ROI). ROI** refers to comparing the training's monetary benefit with the cost of the training—i.e., what do we get for our investment? There are a number of methods for comparing training costs and benefits (usually stated in terms of money, but sometimes stated in terms of performance outcomes) that are probably better left to training practitioners. However, by using the method outlined below and the worksheet on the next page, you can compute a relatively accurate ratio.

Step 1—**Identify outcomes** (e.g., specific quality improvements, a production increase, a reduction in salary/benefit costs, etc.).

Step 2—**Place a value on these outcomes.** Value can be based on employee estimates, or on "hard" data. The value should be reflected in dollars.

Step 3—**Annualize benefits in dollars** by comparing results before and after training (e.g., a production increase of $x$ percent results in an increased annual profit of $x$ dollars, with the production increase the result of training).

Step 4—**Determine the total of all direct and indirect costs.**

Step 5—**Calculate the total savings** by subtracting the training costs from benefits (in dollars).

Step 6—**Calculate ROI** by dividing benefits by costs. This gives you an estimate of the dollar return expected from each dollar invested in training.

# Return on Investment (ROI) Worksheet

## Costs

Program development or purchase (one-time cost) _____

Cost of instructional materials for trainees _____

Cost of instructional materials for trainers _____

Equipment/hardware _____

Facilities _____

Travel/lodging _____

Salary of trainer(s) (including benefits) _____

Support staff salary (including benefits) _____

Cost of lost productivity for attendees (or cost of
   replacement workers) _____

TOTAL COSTS _____

## BENEFITS

Estimated benefit per trainee (in dollars)
$\times$ Number of trainees $\times$ 12 = annual benefit

$ _____ $\times$ _____ $\times$ 12 = _____

$$\text{ROI} = \frac{\text{Return}}{\text{Investment}} = \frac{\text{Benefits}}{\text{Costs}} = \underline{\phantom{xxxxxx}}$$

ROI of 1.0 signifies break-even

ROI of >1.0 signifies a positive return

ROI of <1.0 signifies a negative return

## Training Plan Development

Now that you've examined the underpinnings of successful training, you can begin to develop training plans for each of your employees. The steps outlined below and the accompanying worksheets will provide direction for plan development.

Step 1—With your employee, **review and list organizational goals, objectives, and the training needs** that support them. This will be a review of overall company needs, and operational support needs for your area. Information can be drawn from your earlier Gap Analysis.

Step 2—**List the training needs for the employee's current job,** based on the Gap Analysis.

Step 3—**List the training needs for the employee's desired job(s).**

Step 4—**List any organizational constraints** that you are aware of (funding, political issues, etc.).

Step 5—For each current training need, **list the type of program required,** a possible delivery mode (classroom, computer-based, etc.), expected outcomes, potential sources (in-house, vendor, etc.), and projected unit costs (costs per employee).

## A Training Plan

Employee _____     Date prepared _____

Supervisor _____     Functional Unit _____

| Organizational Goals | Training Needs |
|---|---|
| | |
| | |
| | |
| | |
| | |
| | |
| | |
| | |
| | |

| Organizational Objectives | Training Needs |
|---|---|
| | |
| | |
| | |
| | |
| | |
| | |
| | |
| | |
| | |

| Operational Goals | Training Needs |
|---|---|
| | |
| | |
| | |
| | |
| | |
| | |
| | |
| | |

| Operational Objectives | Training Needs |
|---|---|
|  |  |
|  |  |
|  |  |
|  |  |
|  |  |
|  |  |
|  |  |
|  |  |
|  |  |

Current Employee Training Needs

_____

_____

_____

_____

_____

Future Employee Training Needs

_____

_____

_____

_____

_____

Organizational Constraints

_____

_____

_____

_____

## CURRENT NEEDS

Need _____

Type of Program _____

Delivery Mode _____

Expected Outcomes _____

_____

_____

_____

_____

_____

_____

_____

Potential Sources _____

Projected Unit Cost _____

Need _____

Type of Program _____

Delivery Mode _____

Expected Outcomes _____

_____

_____

_____

_____

_____

_____

_____

Potential Sources _____

Projected Unit Cost _____

Need _____

Type of Program _____

Delivery Mode _____

Expected Outcomes _____

_____

_____

_____

_____

_____

_____

_____


Potential Sources _____

Projected Unit Cost _____

## FUTURE NEEDS

Need _____

Type of Program _____

Delivery Mode _____

Expected Outcomes _____

_____

_____

_____

_____

_____

_____

_____

Potential Sources _____

Projected Unit Cost _____

Need _____

Type of Program _____

Delivery Mode _____

Expected Outcomes _____

_____

_____

_____

_____

_____

_____

_____

Potential Sources _____

Projected Unit Cost _____

61

Need _____

Type of Program _____

Delivery Mode _____

Expected Outcomes _____

_____

_____

_____

_____

_____

_____

_____

Potential Sources _____

Projected Unit Cost _____

**Chapter 4**

# Establishing and Implementing Mentoring Programs

## What is Mentoring?

*Mentoring* can be described in terms of a *relationship* that involves more-experienced employees acting as aides and guides in the learning processes of less-experienced employees. This learning and the consequent behavioral changes that follow is aimed at helping the newer employee succeed in the organization. It's important to note that the definition of "succeed" may vary from organization to organization, depending on the goals and objectives set for the mentoring program.

The more-experienced employee is usually called the *mentor,* while the less-experienced employee is called the *mentee.* Ideally, the mentor helps the mentee become a self-directed learner, able to function successfully on his or her own within the organization. The mentor provides informal training and helps the employee negotiate roadblocks, network, choose formal training, and so on, helping ensure that the socialization process (the process that adapts the employee to the organization's culture) is effective. As we saw in Chapter 1, these activities are some of the very ones that will help a company become a learning organization—one of our ultimate goals.

There are two schools of thought about the mentoring approach to employee development. One school contends that true mentoring is an unplanned, spontaneous series of events that cannot be structured or formalized; it just "happens." According to this school, mentoring is viewed as essentially informal. The other school contends that mentoring is a process that can be controlled, structured, and facilitated. Although mentoring does occur informally, our feeling is that a formal, properly structured program that encompasses training for both mentors and mentees can help create a work environment conducive to self-development and behavioral change that will result in improved job performance. A formal program allows for controlled outcomes that are more likely to prove beneficial to the organization. Most mentoring programs are designed and managed by the Human Resources department; funding for the program varies from organization to organization. If your company already has a mentoring program in place, this chapter will be of use if you see a mentoring role in your future. Our discussion includes a look at mentor and mentee roles, issues of concern to mentees and mentors, tools and strategies you can use to be a more effective mentor, mentoring pitfalls, and keys to relationship-building. If you are already acting as an informal mentor, this chapter will help you be a more effective one. If your company does *not* have a program in place, you may wish to assume a catalyst role if you believe a mentoring system might meet the developmental needs of a significant number of employees. We recommend that you set up a meeting with your Human Resources department to discuss the pros and cons of creating a mentoring system after you have read this chapter.

There is a renewed interest in mentoring, but mentoring activities have been occurring for many centuries. History provides us with a number of examples of mentoring and the value people placed on it. One of the earliest reports of mentoring occured around 1200 B.C. Homer, of Greek fame, tells the story of Odysseus in the *Odyssey*. Before Odysseus left to fight in the Trojan War, he arranged for his trusted friend Mentor to act as guardian and tutor to his son, Telemachus. Homer's story illustrates a practice common in ancient Greece— young males were paired with older males (usually a friend or relative) who acted as role models. The Middle Ages witnessed the rise of craft guilds, where young men were apprentices to a master (a highly skilled craftsman) and eventually became masters themselves. Apprenticeship programs in the skilled trades (the progeny of the craft guilds) still operate today. As we noted earlier, mentoring systems have become more and more important to many companies. They are seen by many as a source of internal regeneration and renewal.

## What is a Mentor?

As noted earlier, a *mentor* acts as teacher, friend, tutor, and advisor to the mentee. The mentor typically performs some or all of the additional functions noted below:

Mentors:

- ◆ Make connections with the "right" people in the organization.

- ◆ Provide or help facilitate organizational rewards.

- ◆ Help the employee understand the organization's culture.

- ◆ Help the employee understand the organization's mission and vision.

- ◆ Provide information on company goals.

- ◆ Act as positive role models.

- ◆ Provide timely and accurate feedback on performance.

- ◆ Provide guidance on how to behave within the context of the organization.

- ◆ Help direct training and education efforts.

- ◆ Provide and direct developmental experiences.

- ◆ Help maintain the relationship with the "natural" boss.

- ◆ Act as confidants, listening to and trying to help with problems mentees are experiencing within the organization.

## The Mentee

The organization selects mentees who have untapped skill sets and who show potential for promotion and receptivity for coaching. The mentee must however, accept responsibility for his or her own development (once again, one of our primary goals). The assessment process described in Chapter 1 can be used to help determine whether or not an employee is a suitable candidate for a mentoring program. If your company already has a program in place and you feel that one or more of your employees will benefit from participation in a program, the Chapter 1 data can help make a case for your employee.

## Stages in the Mentoring Relationship

Table 2 shows the stages of the mentor-mentee relationship. The times associated with each stage are rough approximations.

### Table 2: Stages in the Mentoring Relationship

| Stage | Length of Time | Less-Experienced Employee | More-Experienced Employee |
|---|---|---|---|
| Initiation | 6–12 months | Admires and appreciates the senior employee's competence; he or she is recognized as a source of support and guidance. | Becomes aware that the less-experienced employee is "coachable" and has potential. |
| Cultivation | 2–5 years | Acquires self-confidence, new skills, knowledge, ability to succeed in the organization. Requires less and less support. | Provides developmental opportunities, organizational visibility, protection. |
| Separation | 6–12 months | Becomes autonomous—wants to be independent, but still experiences bouts of anxiety and loss as the independence stage approaches. | Displays competence at developing less-experienced employees as they begin to become more independent. |
| Redefinition | Ongoing | Is grateful for early support and direction, but is no longer dependent. Relationship becomes one of friendship. | Continues to be a supporter and takes pride in the less-experienced employee's accomplishments. Becomes a friend. |

## Mentor Issues

On the plus side, mentors reap a number of benefits. Some of these are noted below:

- **Renewed interest in one's job.** A mentee can bring fresh viewpoints and enthusiasm to a relationship that might carry over to the mentor. The mentor might also have to reflect on how he or she interacts inside the organization, in order to share insights as to what made them successful; this can give the mentor a "second wind."

- **Financial rewards.** Some organizations provide financial rewards for mentors. Your HR department will most likely decide whether compensation is called for (unless you as a manager have input to the establishment of a mentoring program—more on this later in the chapter). Generally, we recommend some type of compensation for senior employees who put in additional time and effort. Our feeling is that compensation also adds to the perceived value of the activity.

- **Increased self-esteem.** This is a very significant benefit. If an individual is asked to be a mentor, he or she is obviously perceived as someone who is knowledgeable and respected, and someone who also probably has skill in managing interpersonal relationships. If a mentor feels better about themselves and is more highly valued by the company, everyone wins—the company, the mentee, and the mentor.

On the negative side, there are factors that might demotivate even the most enthusiastic, committed mentors. Some of these are noted below:

- **Lack of skills.** Mentors must be able to provide timely and accurate performance feedback, and be able provide effective training. He or she should also understand organizational politics as it relates to career planning and be very competent in terms of their own job. Some mentors possess most of the critical mentoring skills, but have never had the occasion to train or tutor. The organization might take steps to help the mentor acquire these skills through formal training or informal on-the-job training (OJT).

- **Inappropriate pressure to be a mentor.** Some years ago, one of the authors was appointed to coordinate a mentoring program. The individual made the mistake of not insisting on a screening program to eliminate unsuitable mentors. Frustration levels rise rapidly when senior employees are pressured into being mentors because of their high-level job performance. This is certainly an important criteria, but some employees might not be psychologically suited to fill a mentoring role for a number of pretty obvious reasons: They might be more concerned about their own careers, they might not feel the need to help less experienced employees, they might feel threatened, and so on. Many people readily adapt to the mentor role, but it is usually a more effective strategy to rely on volunteers, since they are more likely to be committed and enthused. To enhance this role, the organization should take steps to make sure that mentoring is viewed as something special.

◆ **Time and priorities.** Some managers believe that development of their employees is one of their primary responsibilities. Mentors who maintain this stance usually don't have a problem setting aside the necessary time to conduct mentoring activities; *they make it a priority*. If mentors don't hold this view, it is incumbent upon the company to structure the mentoring program in such a way that mentoring *is* viewed as a priority. Meetings should be firmly scheduled and tracked, managers should be permitted extra time to conduct mentoring activities, and mentoring activities should be linked to the performance appraisal of the mentor.

◆ **Payoffs.** We change our behaviors or engage in new behaviors because of payoffs. We also tend to repeat behaviors for which we are rewarded. Human nature is such that unless we receive some reward for behaving a certain way, we won't. Some mentors experience rewards in the form of satisfaction derived from helping less-experienced employees develop. Others need more concrete rewards, and if they don't get them, they might drop out of the program or participate only half-heartedly. Rewards can include public recognition, promotion, bonuses, and performance appraisal benefits. Rewards should be built into the mentoring structure.

◆ **Resentment.** A particularly aggressive mentee who is obviously driven to advance in the organization might be viewed as a threat, especially if the mentor is one level up. Human nature being what it is, some mentors might not participate in the process or they might even throw up roadblocks or sabotage the career of the mentee. It's best to choose mentors who are at least two organizational levels above the mentee.

## Mentoring Strategies, Tools, and Techniques

There are some generally agreed-upon strategies, tools, and techniques that mentors can use to help employees become self-directed developers. Some of the most important are noted below:

◆ **Advice provider.** Providing advice to anyone is sometimes difficult at best. Employees might want to know your thoughts and feelings, but they don't want you to be directive. You should be careful to offer observations, suggestions, and opinions without imposing your solutions. Employees should be encouraged to solve their own problems. If you feel that help is needed but is not being requested, preface your comments with a question such as, "May I offer a suggestion?"

- **The larger view.** Oftentimes, the higher your level in the organization, the broader your perspective. This being the case, a mentor can often provide a mentee with a better understanding of their role and the impact of their job and job performance within the organization.

- **Outside observer.** The mentor is sometimes in the unique position of being able to see things that the mentee is unaware of or is only partially aware of. He or she can share observations related to the work environment, job performance, potential roadblocks, and alternative directions. These observations can often provide insights to the mentee that will greatly help in the employee's developmental effort.

- **Knowledge and experience.** The role of the mentor involves the sharing of often hard-won knowledge and experience—a valuable commodity. This sharing can sometimes help the mentee avoid the same mistakes and pitfalls that might have plagued the mentor early in his or her career. It is natural for a mentor to want the protégé to avoid the same traps he or she fell into, but be careful: Do *not* be directive when you are sharing. Many of us have memories of our parents telling us what to do in a patronizing, lecturing fashion: "When I was your age. . . ." Our reaction is likely to be similar to the one we had when we were teenagers. Rather than *telling,* better strategies are to *suggest,* point out indirectly, tell stories, and relate your experiences. These kinds of strategies can help you share without imposing your solutions to problems, and they will help mentees solve their own problems—one of our developmental goals.

- **Challenges.** A mentor can also provide opportunities for growth by arranging for job assignments that are challenging. It's common practice to set goals that are within reach but pose some level of challenge. Motivation and a sense of accomplishment are enhanced with these types of goals. By providing or arranging for challenging work, you can once again prod your mentee to think for him- or herself and experience feelings of success. By choosing assignments carefully, you can also force employees to go outside their comfort zone and broaden their experience base.

- **Questions.** There are many parallels between selection interviewing and mentoring in terms of the kind of questions you ask and how you ask them.

69

When you conduct a selection interview, you primarily use open-ended questions rather than closed-ended ones. Closed-ended questions are used to confirm a statement or fact, or to obtain specific information: "When were you awarded your MBA?" Open-ended questions, on the other hand, call for an explanation, an opinion, a judgment, and ideas: "What do you feel are the pros and cons of the proposed new system?" As with selection interviewing, try to avoid asking leading questions, such as "Do you think the strategy that I used last year will work?" As we noted in Chapter 2, you should engage your whole self when you listen to the answers to your questions. Active listening strategies apply here, just as they do when you're conducting interviews. You can paraphrase, summarize, and restate by saying, "So, what you're saying is. . . ." You can also probe for the feelings *behind* the words: "It sounds as though you're pretty frustrated with the new reporting relationship." You can also probe for more information: "Tell me more about. . . ." It's also important to use body language (nonverbals) that are perceived as positive (leaning forward, nodding assent, relaxing your body).

If you don't agree with a mentee's idea or you think it is unrealistic, you should provide a measured response. Check your facts: You might not have all the information, or the information might not be accurate. Make sure that you understand completely (active listening). Probe for rationales and likely consequences: "Why did you choose that course of action?" "What might happen if . . . ?" Finally, state your position and concerns, and let the mentee address them.

◆ **The Pygmalion Effect.** One of our favorite phenomena is often referred to as the "Pygmalion effect" or the "Power of expectation." George Bernard Shaw was a prolific playwright and social commentator. *Pygmalion,* one of his early plays, was later used as the basis for the movie *My Fair Lady.* In the movie, Professor Henry Higgins, a linguist, makes a bet that he can pass off the unrefined Eliza Dolittle as a "blueblood" at a royal ball. This presents a challenge, because Eliza is an untutored, uneducated girl selling flowers on the streets of London. Because Professor Higgins believes in Eliza and *expects* her to succeed, she does—duping even another noted linguist.

A number of researchers have investigated this expectation factor by means of experimental studies. The typical experiment involved randomly selecting two study groups from a larger group of students, plant workers, soldiers, etc. The two groups would then attend a class or training session together. The teacher or trainer was told that the members of one group were high-potential workers or gifted students. In reality, the two groups were very much alike, since they had been randomly selected from the same larger group. When the workers or students or soldiers were tested at the end of the program, the participants who were thought by the teacher or trainer to be better performers ended up scoring higher on posttests—sometimes much higher. Since the groups were alike, the variable that probably caused the difference in performance was the *expectation* of the teacher or trainer. Somehow, the teacher or trainer communicated this expectation and affected performance. So, if a mentor *expects* their mentee to succeed, they probably will. The mentor can achieve this effect by consistently thinking in positive terms about the mentee's performance.

This effect is surprisingly powerful. The many experiments that were conducted produced very similar results. It is worth noting that the effect also operates in a negative fashion: If you expect poor performance, the likelihood that you will get just that increases. The Pygmalion effect is obviously just one factor that can influence employee performance, but it might be a very useful tool.

## Mentee Issues

There are, on occasion, problems associated with mentoring systems. Like other systems, they do not always produce the outcomes they were designed for. Sometimes the failure to achieve desired outcomes can be traced to issues that reside with the mentee, and sometimes they can be traced to issues that reside with the mentor but have a negative effect on the mentee. We've noted some of the most common below:

71

- ◆ **The responsibility issue.** At times, mentees do not do a good job of being responsible for their own development. One reason for this is that many organizations foster dependency: they do not reward employees for independent thought, and they often expect employees to check with "higher-ups" before taking action. Some managers, for a myriad of reasons, also have difficulty relinquishing control.

  Some employees lack some of the skills and knowledge required for independent action. Others feel uncomfortable accepting responsibility when they have not been required to do so in the past.

- ◆ **Unkept commitments.** Despite well-designed screening processes, some employees who probably shouldn't become mentors do. Some mentors will miss meetings, delay meetings, not follow through on promises, and so on, causing problems for the mentee. This problem can be minimized by creating a structure that sets up scheduled mentor-mentee interaction and goals and objectives. (More on this later.)

- **Stolen glory.** We've probably all had the experience of someone else taking credit for the work we've done or the ideas that we've had. Every organization has a few employees who will take advantage of new or unsuspecting fellow workers. Mentees should be made aware of the potential for this type of activity and be armed with tools to help them address this kind of situation.

- **Unrealistic expectations.** Mentees (and mentors) should be made aware of the expected outcomes of the program. If promotion is an outcome of participation in the program, then that fact should be clearly stated in the mentoring agreement. If promotion is not a guaranteed outcome, then that fact should be noted. Clear statements of desired program outcomes will help avoid unrealistic expectations.

## Mentee Tips

What follows are tips or guidelines for mentees that can be shared by the mentor. Following these guidelines will help solidify the mentor-mentee relationship and make the mentoring experience more enjoyable and productive for the mentee.

- Both the mentor and mentee should understand that learning is a life-long endeavor. We are never too old, too knowledgeable, or too experienced to cease learning. In fact, in today's world, continuous learning and growth are essential. Mentors must remain open-minded as the relationship develops—after all, mentees also have valuable knowledge to share.

- As we noted earlier, stolen glory ruins work relationships. It is particularly wise to share the glory of mentoring. Everyone benefits if the kudos are passed around.

- Sometimes attitude counts for more than performance. People might not remember who brought that last big contract in, but they will remember how they were treated. As Eliza Dolittle in *My Fair Lady* pointed out, one difference between a lady and a flower girl lies in how they are treated: A flower girl will feel like a lady if she's treated like one.

- Try to find something you have in common beyond the work environment. This will help make the relationship positive and strong.

- Mentors and mentees should think about each other's needs and how the relationship might provide for those needs. To do this, each person must have a solid understanding of the other. Good management practice (really knowing your employees) and effective upward management (really knowing your boss) are important in mentoring relationships.

## The "Natural" Boss

Some problems with mentoring can be traced to a mentee's boss who is not the mentor of that person.

- This boss might not understand the nature, requirements, and benefits of a mentoring system, and might feel that the employee is avoiding his or her "real" work.

- The boss might be jealous or envious of the mentee's relationship with a mentor who is two or three levels up. The boss might feel that the mentee has access to knowledge that he or she is not privy to. After all, knowledge *is* power.

- Some bosses lack commitment to the mentoring program. They might feel that the resources being expended could be better used elsewhere.

- Some bosses might not place much stock in the idea of controlled employee development, feeling that employees should develop themselves without any assistance.

Building bridges between the natural boss, the mentee, and the mentor will help ensure that your company's mentoring program will run smoothly. Listed below are some bridge-building strategies:

- The mentoring system structure should provide for formal, scheduled interaction between the mentor and the natural boss.

- The natural boss should observe and participate in the mentoring program orientation.

- Use the natural boss's knowledge of the mentee. The natural boss can provide insight into the mentee's knowledge, skills, needs, and job performance. When the mentoring agreement is drawn up, the natural boss can provide data to the mentor or actively participate in the process.

- The mentor, mentee, and natural boss should meet periodically to discuss issues related to the mentoring effort (performance planning, learning opportunities, networking opportunities, etc.).

## Mentoring System Models

There are many mentoring system models in use today. It is beyond the scope of this book to provide examples and descriptions of the different types of models. Figure 7 describes what a typical program might look like in terms of the flow of major activities. An explanation of these major activities follows the flowchart.

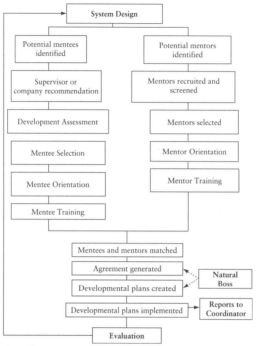

**Figure 7:** A Mentoring System

## A Mentoring System

**System design.** The first step in our model involves the evaluation and selection of a mentoring system that will suit the purposes of your organization. A good place to start this investigation is on the Web. Using the keyword "mentoring," you can locate organizations that have put mentoring programs in place. Most organizations will share their experiences with you or your Human Resources department. There are, of course, many mentoring books, articles, and videotapes available from local libraries. You can also employ a vendor to help with program design.

**Caution.** Before the organization starts the search, it might be helpful to take a little time to think about what the objectives for your program are (to establish a pipeline of skilled employees, to help in succession planning, to improve organizational learning capability, and so on).

### Choosing and Preparing Mentors

**Identify potential mentees.** One approach to mentee selection is to begin with a database of all potential program participants and then narrow the list, based on the goals and objectives set for the program. For example, you might wish to target women managers who could be groomed to move up. You might decide to open up the process and make it self-nominating and egalitarian in nature so that all employees have an equal chance of being selected. Whatever process your company decides to use, it should be widely understood. All employees should be aware of the purpose of and rationale for the program. Employees who are not identified in this initial stage should understand why they were not chosen. Time spent up front helping your employees become aware can smooth the path of program implementation and prevent or minimize hard feelings later on.

**Supervisor or company recommendations.** Your nomination system can be set up in several ways: Supervisors might be requested to submit candidate names; the company might request employees to participate; other sponsors might submit names; the organization might use a competitive process.

**Developmental assessment.** The assessment process can vary. You can use relatively simple instruments, such as Assessment 1 (in Chapter 1), or use complex Assessment Center operations, where employees participate in a one- or two-week assessment process, facilitated by trained assessors. An Assessment Center can provide data related to an employee's decision-making skills, their management styles, management knowledge and skills, company and industry knowledge, domain knowledge, and so on. Data related to developmental needs might also be garnered from performance appraisals, self-reports, peer reports, and supervisory reports. Whatever the source of developmental data, the needs that are identified should be prioritized and an initial development plan created.

**Mentee selection.** This step involves the selection of employees into the program. All the employees who have been assessed can be chosen, or the company can limit participations. The company might have to establish a rotation based on selection criteria such as organizational need, available mentors who are suitable matches, and the resources that can be committed to the program.

**Mentee orientation.** Once the initial group of mentees is selected, schedule an orientation session. In this session, mentees can be further apprised of the nature of the program, the expectations that exist for them, how much time might be required, their potential relationship with the "natural boss," and so on.

**Mentee training.** This step can be lengthy and involved, depending on the skills possessed by the mentee. An assessment of training needs can be conducted during the original mentee assessment process. Training topics might include managing interpersonal relationships, managing upward, goal setting, and seeking feedback.

## Choosing and Preparing Mentors

**Potential mentors identified.** Creating a database of potential mentors can be difficult. Senior employees might be reluctant to be included in a database, and information about potential mentors can be lacking. There is also a risk of overlooking employees who would make exemplary mentors (internal politics, lack of personal knowledge about the potential mentor, etc.). Mentors can be identified by other managers, mentees, or Human Resources, or they can volunteer. If potentially good mentors are overlooked, they can join the program at a later date.

**Mentors recruited and screened.** Mentors can volunteer, be recruited by senior managers, or be approached by a mentee or Human Resources. A screening system usually involves a selection committee and/or the program coordinator. The most important questions to be answered are: "Is this person willing to do all that is required of a mentor?" and "Does this candidate possess the requisite skills to be an effective mentor?"

**Mentors selected.** Mentors are selected to participate based on their potential personal compatibility with a small number of mentees and their ability to help the mentees develop in the areas that were identified in the mentee Developmental Assessment phase.

**Mentor orientation.** In the orientation session, mentors are apprised of the time that will be required, what types of activities they will be expected to participate in, reporting requirements, budget constraints, and so on.

**Mentor training.** Training will depend on the skills of the mentor and the resources that might be available for training. Topics might include how to provide timely and accurate feedback, conduct one-on-one meetings, and manage interpersonal relationships.

## Program Implementation

**Mentees and mentors are matched.** This step involves the final match of mentors to individual employees. The match can be based on the desires of the mentees, the developmental needs of mentees, the suitability of the mentor in terms of being able to provide what a given mentee needs, and the perceived compatibility of personalities.

**Agreement is generated.** Although an agreement might be informal, we recommend that it be formalized. Agreements, goals, objectives, and action plans stand a better chance of being carried out if they are laid out on paper. The agreement should include a confidentiality statement; meeting requirements between the mentee, mentor, natural boss, and program coordinator; the time to be invested in the program; specific duties of the mentor and mentee; and the approximate duration of the relationship. To give you an idea of what an agreement form looks like, we have provided a sample at the end of the chapter.

**Developmental plans created.** Action plans for each developmental goal of the mentee should be developed, consisting of goal worksheets with projected completion dates, required and potential resources, potential roadblocks, and reporting requirements. We have provided a sample plan at the end of the chapter.

**Developmental plans implemented.** In this step, the mentor and mentee work to complete the developmental plans within the parameters established in the mentoring agreement. Progress reports should be submitted to the program coordinator on a predetermined schedule. These reports represent the minimum established in the original program design. The coordinator might request additional data at any time.

**Note:** If the mentor is not the mentee's "natural boss," the mentor should participate in or at least observe the development of the mentoring agreement and the creation of the developmental plans.

**Evaluation.** As the program progresses, it should be evaluated on a number of measures. These should include a cost-benefit analysis to help determine the value of the program to the company. The evaluation plan should also include measurement of the achievement of the goals and objectives initially established for the program. Questions to ask: Is the program accomplishing what you originally envisioned? Is the program cost-effective? Is the system operating as planned?

## Mentor-Mentee Relationship Issues

There are a number of relationship issues that should be considered when creating a mentoring system. Some of the most important are discussed below:

- ◆ **Gender.** The potential for sexual attraction, regardless of their role in the relationship, is a fact of corporate life. There is probably little that can be done to eliminate the potential for personal involvement, but there are a few steps you should consider to help minimize problems. Review the company's policies on sexual issues and relationships that are strictly forbidden. Discuss the possible consequences of the violation of company policies. Discuss the nature of and potential for sexual attraction in the mentoring relationship. Provide recourse for both parties if either behaves inappropriately.

- ◆ **Needs.** Responsibilities, roles, and goals can be explicitly laid out, but there will be occasions when a mentee feels that his or her needs are not being met through this mentoring relationship. The mentor can suggest that the program coordinator serve as a sounding board to help illuminate the mentee's concerns. The mentor might also suggest that the mentee write down his or her concerns on paper as a starting point for further discussion and resolution.

◆ **Cross-cultural issues.** As we are all well aware, the American workforce is becoming increasingly diverse. It's easy to see how some matches won't work out. There is sometimes a concern when trying to match employees from different cultural backgrounds. We are who we are, partly because of where, when, and how we were raised to maturity. We tend to identify with people who were raised in similar circumstances. You're probably aware that this is an ongoing issue in employee selection—we tend to want to employ people *who are like us*. We could spend a great deal of time examining cross-cultural issues, but we're limited by the scope of this book; suffice to say that most such problems can be minimized by *honesty and understanding*. Whether this understanding comes from workshops, independent study by the mentor, or advice from other managers who understand the culture in question, the key is to be able, at least to some degree, to put yourself in the other employee's shoes. We can never hope to fully understand another culture, but we can prepare ourselves to address cross-cultural issues as they arise.

## Special Considerations

There are a number of issues and concerns that are of particular importance to mentors, senior managers, and Human Resources. Let's start with one very important one:

◆ **A key concern.** As with many organizational initiatives, top management support is critical to the successful implementation of a mentoring system. It is incumbent upon Human Resources to ensure that upper management and key stakeholders understand the concept of mentoring, potential costs of the program, and potential benefits to the organization, mentors, and mentees.

Additional Issues and Concerns

1. The collection of demographic data related to the workforce is necessary in order to obtain a comprehensive picture of the mentor pool, the mentee pool, and organizational needs.

2. Mentor and mentee screening and selection criteria development should be

by cross-functional committee. This approach will help avoid biases and improve program support across the organization.

3. A program evaluation plan should be developed as part of the original system design.

4. The question of why the mentoring program is needed should be answered early on (cross-training, upward mobility, succession planning, promotion, improvement of organizational capabilities, and so on).

5. As with all goals, expected program outcomes should be stated in measurable, specific terms.

6. Potential training programs for both mentees and mentors should be planned for and budgeted for.

7. To help ensure long-term success, develop an ongoing internal marketing program (use newsletters, e-mails, team meetings, organization-wide meetings, communications from upper management, and so on).

8. Decide early on how the program costs will be handled.

9. Provide coordinator training.

10. Consider doing a pilot, just as you would for a training program.

11. Establish a system for dealing with program exits. Mentors or mentees might leave the program for any number of reasons (transfer, other employment, new work obligations, and so on).

12. Human Resources can provide individual performance insights and perspective not available elsewhere in the organization.

13. Devise a reporting and tracking system that is easy to use and that does not require an inordinate amount of time.

14. Allow sufficient time to establish the system—it might take six months or more.

15. Create and publicize a mentor reward system.

## Mentoring Forms

The remainder of the chapter consists of sample forms that you can modify or use as-is.

## A Mentoring Agreement

We are entering into a mentor-mentee relationship that we expect will produce benefits for us and the company. The focus of our relationship will be achievement of the goals stated in the developmental plan created for the employee (noted below). We will work *together* to achieve stated developmental goals and objectives while meeting the company's goals.

The nature of and activities related to our relationship will be confidential. Information about the relationship will be shared only with the expressed consent of both parties to the relationship.

We understand the nature of the mentoring relationship and agree to it in spirit and in form.

We agree to terminate the relationship if either party deems that action to be appropriate.

Details of the agreement are outlined below.

Mentee _____     Mentor _____
(PLEASE PRINT)

Expectations for the Mentor:

_____

_____

_____


Expectations for the Mentee:

_____

_____

_____


Approximate time to be devoted by the Mentor to mentoring activities:

_____

_____

_____

Mentee-Mentor meeting schedule and duration:

_____

_____

Approximate duration of the relationship:

_____

"Natural" boss meeting schedule (if applicable):

_____

Additional points for agreement:

_____

_____

_____

_____


_____          _____

Signature of Mentor                        Date

_____          _____

Signature of Mentee                        Date

## Mentee Profile

Name _____ Current position _____

Official title/grade _____ Employment date _____

Contact information: _____

_____

_____

Reports to: _____ Official title/grade _____

Contact information: _____

_____

_____

Education level _____

Schools attended

    High School: _____

       College: _____

    University: _____

Summary of most recent performance appraisal:

_____

_____

_____

_____

_____

Special skills:

_____

_____

_____

Special knowledge/certifications:

_____

_____

_____

Professional association memberships:

_____

_____

_____

Publications in field:

_____

_____

_____

Information from superior, Human Resources, other managers regarding job performance, relationship skills, motivators, perceived capabilities, limitations:

_____

_____

_____

_____

_____

83

## The Development Plan

Mentee _____          Mentor _____

Date _____

**REMEMBER:** Each developmental goal should be stated in specific, measurable terms.

Developmental goal _____

Skills and knowledge I expect to acquire by achieving this goal:

_____

_____

_____

_____

Learning activities that will help me acquire the knowledge and skills required to reach my goal:

_____

_____

_____

_____

Resources that might be required to help me achieve my goal:

_____

_____

_____

Roadblocks or barriers that might prevent me from achieving my goal:

_____

_____

_____

_____

Indicators: I will know I have achieved my goal when . . .

_____

| Action Steps | Target Completion Dates | Status / Comments |
|---|---|---|
|  |  |  |

# Coaching and Development

## What is a Coach?

In our view, a coach is primarily a *partner*—someone who brings common interests, common goals, and trust to an association or relationship. You and your employees are natural candidates for a coaching relationship because you share common interests and goals: You have significant career investments. You ultimately share elements of the same resource pool. It's a win-win situation if you and your employees succeed in your jobs. You face many similar challenges in your work environment. And, if the organization succeeds, the chances are better that both of you will succeed.

You can build a very positive relationship with your employees by using coaching as a tool. If you work to create a motivating environment, solve problems together, and work at creating trust between the two of you, a strong bond will be established that will help see the both of you through stormy organizational seas.

We also see coaching as a process, not a single event—a process designed to improve performance over time. Some managers conceptualize coaching as an event or unrelated series of events that occur when a performance issue arises or some organizational roadblock must be addressed. Coaching involves guided, incremental change; you can't change overnight, and neither can your employees. Change and improvement in job performance occurs slowly, over time. Managers who are willing to devote time and effort over an extended period will achieve better long-term results than managers who don't treat coaching as an event and allow the coaching process to evolve and grow.

## Trust that Binds

Trust between the coach and the employee is the glue that holds the coaching relationship together. All managers are very aware that without trust, effective management is an uphill struggle. This being the case, we felt that a discussion of the coaching process should begin with a look at the nature of trust and how trust is created and nurtured.

Trust is a two-way street: It depends on open, honest communication. Both parties must be convinced that if they are honest and open, they will not be criticized unjustly—they should both expect honest feedback. Trust provides a safe, confidential "space" for both the employee and the manager. Both parties must also feel that they can depend on the other party to consistently follow through. Following through consistently doesn't have to be based on major commitments. Being on time for coaching sessions, following through on small promises, and returning calls or e-mails in a timely fashion can all lay the groundwork for a trusting relationship. In addition to facilitating and holding a coaching relationship together, trust also:

- ◆ Improves productivity
- ◆ Increases commitment levels
- ◆ Increases respect levels
- ◆ Improves the working environment
- ◆ Helps improve morale

Many of the communication guidelines that should be followed when managing any change process should also be followed when striving to improve trust levels:

- ◆ Tell people the truth as you know it, even if it's bad news.
- ◆ Be as clear as you can.
- ◆ Use active listening techniques to be sure that you are communicating accurately.
- ◆ Share information continually through both formal and informal channels.
- ◆ Share information face-to-face when possible.
- ◆ Ask appropriate clarifying questions so that both parties clearly understand the other's position and concerns.

In addition to maintaining open communication channels and continually communicating, you can improve trust levels by making sure that employees are given the credit they deserve. Be sure to admit that you are human, too (when you make mistakes). It's also important to address problems as soon as they arise: Focus on the facts. Give employees the benefit of the doubt. Assume that until proven otherwise, the employee is doing their best. Don't assign blame; it doesn't help solve the problem—it just builds resentment. You should also provide employees with opportunities to prove that they can be trusted.

## A Coaching Process

There are many coaching models you can choose from to direct your coaching efforts. We offer the one described below:

Step 1—**Build an open, supportive relationship.** This step is a necessary precursor because without an open relationship that is perceived by the employee as being supportive, anything else you do is likely to be ineffectual or resisted by the employee. In a coaching environment, employees must feel relatively safe. Some supportive behaviors that you can employ are listed below:

- If a performance issue arises, assume some of the responsibility. Odds are that you might have contributed in some way to the problem. Even if you haven't, your employee will appreciate the sentiment.

- As with any performance discussion, use the "sandwich" technique: Sandwich any negative discussion between positive comments about past performances and positive comments about expected future performance.

- Recognize and explain the employee's current and future value to the organization.

- Stress that you and the employee are partners in the performance improvement quest.

- Listen with your whole self. Engage the employee. Use nonverbals: lean forward, remove physical communication barriers like tables and chairs, widen your eyes, and nod assent. Be sure to acknowledge their concerns and feelings.

- Keep the exchange positive. Be warm, open, empathetic, and nonjudgmental.

89

◆ Spend a few minutes talking about the employee's needs, dreams, and wishes.

Step 2—**Define and delimit the relationship.** This step involves a discussion of the roles and responsibilities of each partner. It's important that each partner understand his or her contribution to the relationship and any limitations required by the relationship. For example, each party must understand the need to openly communicate with, be truthful with, and trust their partner. The coach should also consider and then explain what he or she is willing to do in terms of helping out, providing resources (or access to resources), and offering one-on-one consult time.

Step 3—**Define performance issues and problems.** One of the most important steps in the problem-solving process is to *clearly define* the problem before considering possible solutions. One strategy is to define *the gap* between current and desired performance, determine why it might exist, and specify what the cause(s) might be. This is especially important in a performance discussion—you must determine the true root causes for performance discrepancies. If you focus on inappropriate or incorrect causes, the whole coaching effort will be jeopardized. It's important that you describe the issues and your concerns in a non-threatening, business-like way without any hint of recrimination. You must focus on the facts as you know them. Voice your concerns and then ask your employee to restate them in their own words to help eliminate any chance of misinterpretation.

One of the goals of this step is to eliminate misunderstandings so that both you and the employee know exactly where each other stands. This is the point where you explain what you expect to happen in terms of changed behaviors. It is extremely important that the employee understand what is expected of them. You cannot expect the employee to read your mind. Be specific. Ask for a restatement of your comments.

Step 4—**Consider current behaviors and their impact.** Before your employee can choose alternative or new behaviors to replace current behaviors, they must consider the impact that current behaviors are having on their performance. Self-awareness is key to any type of behavioral change. This step presents a golden opportunity for you to help your employees increase their self-awareness and enhance their buy-in to the coaching process. While providing direction and encouragement, you allow employees to discover, on their own, what impact their current behaviors are having. A good strategy is to ask the employee to list the costs and benefits associated with their current actions. You might also ask the employee to consider the means they are currently using to reach certain ends. Ask if and how well those means are working for them. Any time spent at this stage is well worth it. There is a tendency in our fast-paced environments to want to rush forward and create goals and action plans. If you allow employees *time* to discover the impact of their current behaviors and think about what kinds of outcomes alternative behaviors might produce, they will be much more likely to be enthused about and committed to new directions.

Step 5—**Revisit values and career goals.** As we noted in Chapter 2, values are one determinant of behavior and the shape and nature of career goals. Since our values shape both behavior and goals, we feel that it is important for the employee to review his or her values and determine if they are compatible with new work behaviors and performance goals. If they are not compatible, the employee might wish to rethink the means they use to achieve work ends. Perhaps alternative approaches can be devised. It is also important that performance goals contribute to the achievement, at least to some degree, of career goals. Remember, employee development should be viewed as an ongoing *multi-level process,* and all developmental activities and strategies are ultimately interrelated.

Step 6—**Formulate goals.** It is important to remember when completing this step that employees must be intimately involved in goal setting. There is a tendency among some managers to set goals and then obtain employee consent. You are a partner in performance improvement. Partners work together to achieve mutually desired ends. Involve employees as much as possible. As with any goals, performance goals need to be clear, understood by everyone, and realistic. It is worth noting that a number of studies have found that clear, difficult (but not too difficult), specific goals are more likely to be reached than unclear, easy-to-reach goals.

Step 7—**Consider roadblocks and barriers.** As with career planning, planning for performance improvement should include an evaluation of potential roadblocks and barriers. There are, however, some roadblocks and barriers that are not within the power of the employee to overcome. As a manager, you can help the employee surmount these obstacles by having discussions with other managers to smooth a path, providing access to resources, and acting as a sounding board to discuss and help resolve issues like procedural problems and resource allocation.

Step 8—**Consider the consequences of behavioral changes.** A discussion of the positive consequences of behavioral change allows you to reinforce the need for change and improve employee commitment levels. Step 4 provided an opportunity for employees to realistically assess the impact of their current way of doing things. This step allows them to revisit alternative behaviors and further define how change will benefit *them*. This step also provides you with an opportunity to point out potential benefits that they might have overlooked or been unaware of.

Step 9—**Create an employee action plan.** You and your employee should work together to formulate a doable action plan. Some negotiation might be required, but negotiation is a positive activity. If employees feel they have played a significant role in creating a plan that they will be charged with implementing, they are much more likely to be committed to it. It is also important that the employee *verbalize* a commitment. You and the employee must be clear on the expectations that exist for both partners. In addition, you should be certain that the employee truly believes the plan can be carried out within the established timelines.

Step 10—**Establish a follow-up plan.** Your follow-up plan is critical to long-term success. The most effective coaches are those who have the most contact with their employees to discuss their progress. Follow-up sessions also allow for changes in direction as conditions change. If your employee views you as being committed, he or she is likely to be committed. It is also important that you are accessible on a regular basis. You should use these sessions to evaluate and possibly improve your processes—that is, the way that you manage the coaching relationship. It might also be helpful to construct a "scorecard" that will allow each party to rate the effectiveness of the other and rate the progress of the relationship.

**Reminder:** Coaching is a process, not an event. The process described above, if it is to be as effective as possible, must take place over time, with multiple meetings scheduled.

Now that we have examined a coaching process, we will turn our attention to some individual issues that we have not yet discussed, qualities and skills possessed by effective coaches, and session management skills and guidelines. We will also examine the coaching-performance appraisal link.

## Individual Issues

A coach must keep in mind that the primary focus of coaching is the employee. The performance of the work unit is important, of course, but the employee must be the central driving force. All employees seek a certain amount of fulfillment from their jobs. Performance improvement strategies should reflect personal driving forces in addition to values. Employees also desire some measure of balance in their lives. This idea is important in career planning, but it should also be considered in performance planning. The desire for balance might affect how much time and effort an employee is willing to devote to performance improvement.

There are a number of human needs and concerns that should be kept in mind as you carry out the coaching process. Some of these are described below:

- Many people identify with their jobs and careers. It is important to keep performance issues in the proper perspective. One incident does not make a career. A job does not define a person.

- Performance discussions might result in or lead to emotional outbursts. Employees might feel threatened or may be concerned about their future, their value to the company, and their worth as individuals. Take the time to determine what your employees are really concerned about and emotionally invested in.

- Conflict is often associated with performance issues. Oftentimes the conflict is fact based—disagreement exists over how parties *perceive* what the facts are. Facts might seem to be facts to one person, but not another. Perception is reality. At times, as we noted earlier, conflict is also value-based.

- Self-confidence can be damaged during coaching activities. It is important to remember that we all have egos, some of which are more easily damaged than others. Commitment to change might be difficult to accomplish due to ego issues. Maintain a positive tone during *all* discussions.

## The Effective Coach

The most effective coaches possess certain skills and personal characteristics, and exhibit behaviors that are conducive to effective coaching. Of course, no one individual can possibly possess them all, but coaches can engage in their own self-development activities to become the best coach they can be. Listed below are skills that can be acquired, characteristics that can be fostered, and behaviors that can be employed to help increase the effectiveness of your coaching effort.

- The ability to "connect" at more than a superficial level will facilitate the coaching process. As a coach, you should focus on *really* getting to know your employee professionally, and you should also allow your employee to know you professionally. Get to know each other outside the boundaries of formal work relationships (formal position in the company hierarchy and job title). What drives each of you? What motivates each of you? What values do you share? This knowledge will allow you both to better appreciate the uniqueness and value that you each bring to the company. It will also allow you to view each other as distinct human beings with your own set of needs and wants.

♦ Listening occurs at different levels. At one level, we hear the words people are saying and attach meaning to them. At a deeper level, we look for the meaning *behind* the words. The meaning behind the words can be better understood by considering the nonverbal elements of messages—conversational tone and pace, emotional signals, and the like. The effective coach looks for comments that do not ring true and for inconsistencies, hesitation, mixed feelings, negative or positive body language, etc. The path to effective listening lies with really understanding your employees. This, once again, involves devoting the necessary time and effort; relationships are not built overnight.

♦ Effective coaches understand the need for absolute confidentiality. As we noted earlier, employees need a "safe zone" where they can explore options, talk freely about their concerns and issues, and engage in personal discovery. You can help create a safe zone by consistently encouraging and praising openness, by being nonjudgmental, and by acknowledging your employee's efforts. It is important that you address the confidentiality issue early in the process, since you will both be seeking open and honest communication. This will come more easily if your employee feels comfortable in the relationship. The agreement between you and your employee should be precise and specific: "I, as your coach, will not reveal to anyone what we say during our sessions without your specific permission." You might wish to adopt the process guidelines described later in the chapter.

♦ As we noted earlier, effective coaches are able to connect at more than a superficial level. They are also adept at maintaining friendly relationships by doing the little things you might think of as politeness and respect: apologizing when late for a meeting, and not accepting phone calls during a session, for example.

♦ Effective coaches also continually monitor the coaching relationship. Whatever you choose to call them—reviews, updates, touch-base sessions, and so on—the coach should take the time to track progress, head off problems, and maintain motivation for change.

♦ The most successful coaches are also proactive. They do not sit back and wait for problems to appear or opportunities for positive reinforcement to become obvious. They remain on the lookout for possible roadblocks and barriers to forward progress and opportunities for praising the efforts of their employees.

## Feedback

Giving accurate, timely, and specific feedback on a frequent basis is critical to effective coaching. Feedback provides many positives for employees. Some of these are listed below:

◆ Employees receive guidance that helps them continually adjust their behavior based on changing work environments.

◆ Feedback, especially positive feedback, indicates to employees that they are important organizational players—what they do and how they perform has a significant organizational impact.

◆ Honest feedback helps build and solidify the coach-employee relationship.

◆ Feedback helps coaching partners stay focused on performance issues.

◆ Feedback helps employees steadily and progressively modify performance.

Feedback can also have negative consequences. Research conducted in recent years indicates that most employees do not like to be micromanaged (too much feedback), do not like too much negative feedback, would like more positive feedback, do not receive enough feedback in general, receive feedback that is not specific enough, and receive feedback too long after an inappropriate or ineffective behavior has occurred. To have the greatest impact on behavioral change, feedback should occur as soon as possible after a behavior is displayed. Tips for providing timely feedback are listed below:

◆ Provide on-the-spot feedback whenever the occasion presents itself. Immediate feedback is powerful. Its effect is much more pronounced than feedback a day or two or three after the fact.

◆ Try to visualize potential future opportunities for feedback, and set aside time in your schedule to provide it. Your employees will soon sense that you are serious about contributing to their success.

◆ Set deadlines for yourself. Feedback activities sometimes have a way of getting put on the back burner when other job responsibilities present themselves. Review your feedback activities weekly. Try not to let a week go by without providing some input to your employees.

◆ Set aside a little time every day *at the same time* to provide feedback. This will increase the chances that you will carry through on a consistent basis.

◆ Develop a standardized *process* for feedback requests. Employees are more likely to request feedback if they have a formalized way of requesting it that remains the same from request to request.

◆ Use the time you have set aside for feedback wisely. Get to the point quickly without appearing too abrupt. Both partners are more likely to value the feedback experience if they feel that the time is being wisely spent.

◆ Make sure that the feedback you provide is concise and readily understood. If employees do not have to deal with vague feedback, they will be able to take action more quickly.

## The Outstanding Performer

Some managers will fall prey to human nature and shy away from coaching those employees who are outstanding performers. This is understandable not to want to upset an employee who consistently performs at an above-average level. Managers sometimes assume that these employees do not need or want to be coached. On the contrary, it is our feeling that *all* employees, on occasion, want and need coaching. We all need to be paid attention to, feel appreciated, and be valued as contributors to the organization's success. And, no matter how excellent a performer we are, we will occasionally have problems with performance.

You have probably noticed that high performers have the requisite knowledge, skills, and abilities to do their jobs, and that they are usually intrinsically motivated and driven to succeed. Performance shortcomings are probably not linked to the reasons we discussed earlier, but rather to not understanding the assignment, not realizing an assignment should have been approached differently, or not having proper access to organizational resources. These issues need to be addressed, but you can take a more collaborative, supportive, low-key approach to a problem that will minimize the risk of making a high-level performer feel attacked, undervalued, and unappreciated. One last caution here: Be straightforward. Top performers are top performers because they are intelligent and perceptive. They will quickly determine if you are beating around the bush or trying to avoid unpleasant issues.

## Coaching vs. Performance Appraisal

At times, some managers get confused about the differences between coaching and performance appraisal. Appraisals can provide opportunities for coaching activities, and coaching activities might produce data that is helpful in appraisal, but these two performance management tools are fundamentally different. To help eliminate any confusion between the two, we have described some of these differences below:

- Coaching seeks changes in employee behavior by the use of a collaborative, supportive approach based on open, two-way communication. The aim is to help the employee discover their own underlying performance issues and, in concert with the coach, establish new directions and acquire new, more-effective work behaviors. As we noted earlier, coaching is an ongoing process that takes place over time and seeks to change behavior progressively and incrementally. Appraisal is just what the term intimates—*appraisal* of performance based on a manager's perceptions. It is often a subjective assessment of an employee's progress and relative value to the company, usually conducted once or twice a year.

- Coaching aims at taking advantage of developmental opportunities as they occur. The coaching mindset is a proactive one. Appraisal aims at providing information to management to help determine the distribution of rewards and punishment. It is reactive in the sense that it occurs after the fact—judgments are made after the performance has occurred. Goals are set for the upcoming appraisal period and are often not reviewed or evaluated until the next appraisal.

- The coaching process provides for frequent, immediate feedback that centers on what is happening now. Appraisal provides for infrequent feedback, often provided long after the performance or nonperformance has occurred.

- The coach is most concerned about partnering with employees to define and solve problems with a view toward individual development and the seamless integration of employee needs with organizational needs. Appraisal involves the documentation of employee strengths and weaknesses in relation to preset organizational goals and objectives and strives to integrate employee objectives with work group objectives.

## Building Commitment

Whatever performance level your employees are at—average, below average, or outstanding—commitment to performance improvement is critical. If employees are not committed to change, it is likely to be an uphill battle. We have listed below some strategies that are commonly used to build commitment:

- **Empowerment.** True empowerment is a powerful force. When employees are given authority along with responsibility and have been adequately trained, their results will be superior and you will be fulfilling some of their basic human needs—the need to achieve, to be all they can be, to be thought of as a valuable contributor, and so on. Empowerment leads to increased commitment.

◆ **Direction.** When employees feel they have direction and focus, they are more likely to be committed. Reaching any goal requires that you understand why and where you are headed and what is expected of you. This knowledge will help provide a driving force.

◆ **Participation.** Employees are more likely to become involved contributors if they feel that they have a say in day-to-day matters. Providing mechanisms for employee input into planning, problem solving, and decision making can reap huge commitment rewards.

◆ **Appreciation.** We all react strongly to demonstrations of gratitude from our peers, our superiors, and our subordinates. Whether the show of gratitude is formal or informal doesn't really matter, except in the case of the employee who might be embarrassed by formal public displays. In that case, a private show of appreciation is probably called for.

## Managing Diversity

There are many competing definitions of diversity and prescriptions for dealing with it in the workplace. Simply put, it relates to the differences and similarities among people. As you might imagine, we could engage in an extensive discussion of the impact of similarities and differences on workforce performance. Instead, let's review assumptions that could put a crimp in your coaching plans. We all know that these assumptions are false, but we can fall prey to them if we aren't careful. Some of these assumptions are noted below:

◆ **Stereotyping.** This assumption involves thinking that persons who belong to a different group than you (religious, political, ethnic, sexual orientation, gender, etc.) are all relatively the same in terms of their thinking and behavior. They're not.

◆ **Setting low expectations.** This assumption often builds off of stereotyping. The assumption is that if an employee belongs to this or that group, they are not very capable, are not willing to work hard, etc. Not so.

◆ **Differences are negative.** This assumption involves believing that "they" have nothing in common with "us" and that we will never understand their way of thinking and behaving. Not so.

◆ **Sameness is equality.** Some managers assume that if you manage all your employees the same way, you are managing them equally. People do have different needs. Different management and coaching strategies based on these differing needs are necessary if you are going to establish an effective partnership.

## Preparing for a Coaching Meeting

Meetings are more likely to achieve their purpose if they are planned. A planned meeting is also usually more focused and consumes less time. We have listed some questions you can ask yourself and some activities you can undertake to help your coaching meetings go more smoothly:

1. Set aside uninterrupted time. Choose a meeting site where you are not likely to be disturbed for the entire meeting time.

2. Think about the objectives for the meeting. What outcomes are you seeking? Share them with your employee.

3. Think about your own preparation. What do you plan to do? Ask questions? Provide information? Preparation is key.

4. Think about your employee's preparation. What do you want them to be prepared to do? Share your expectations.

5. Create an agenda replete with topics and times, but leave a cushion for unexpected changes in direction or unforeseen topics.

6. Plan for the next meeting or follow-up activity.

## Coaching Forms

Four worksheets are provided in this chapter. The first is designed to help you think about the coaching process you might soon begin. The next two are designed for the employee: One is a change assessment, and the other is an action-planning document related to goal setting. The fourth is a tracking form document to help you monitor your coaching activities.

# A Pre-Coaching Planner

*This planning guide is designed to help you prepare for the coaching process. By answering the questions stated below, you will be better prepared to manage the coaching process.*

Employee _____     Date _____

1. Is this employee someone who will be amenable to and participate in the coaching process? Will he or she do well in a partnering relationship? Why? Why not?

   _____

   _____

   _____

   _____

2. Make a list of reasons why it is important for this employee to change his or her current behaviors. What advantage(s) will be gained by the employee?

   _____

   _____

   _____

   _____

   _____

   _____

   _____

3. What will happen if this employee does not respond to your coaching efforts? Have you spoken with someone in Human Resources to explore the likelihood of this being the case?

   _____

   _____

   _____

4.  Describe or list your own expectations for the employee as they relate to resolving the situation.

    _____

    _____

    _____

    _____

    _____

    _____

5.  Describe the situation as you see it. Be specific.

    _____

    _____

    _____

    _____

    _____

**101**

## Change Assessment

*Completing this change assessment will help you create a viable action plan.*

| Types of Changes | Current Situation | Desired Change(s) | Results if Change Occurs | Results if Change Does Not Occur |
|---|---|---|---|---|
| *Personal* | | | | |
| *Interpersonal* | | | | |
| *Organizational* | | | | |

## Setting Goals for Action

Name _____   Date _____

*Goals are reached by taking some sort of action. Actions are hindered or enhanced by certain factors. The questions below will help you think about these factors and how your performance goals might best be reached. Guidelines for establishing or setting goals are also listed.*

Goals must be:

- **Specific.** Goals must be specifically and clearly stated.

- **Measurable.** Goals must lend themselves to measurement, if possible.

- **Achievable.** Goals should be difficult, but still be attainable.

- **Realistic.** Goals must be achievable, given the available skills, knowledge, and abilities of individuals or teams trying to reach them. Adequate resources must also be available.

- **Timed.** Time limits for completion should accompany goals.

1. My performance goal is _____

2. This goal will be accomplished by _____

3. How important is it to you to reach this goal? What will happen when you reach your goal? What will happen if you don't reach your goal?

   _____

   _____

   _____

4. What personal strengths and resources do you have that will help you reach your goal?

   _____

   _____

   _____

**103**

5. What organizational resources do you have access to that will help you reach your goal?

_____

_____

_____

_____

6. What other personal or organizational resources will be needed for you to reach your goal?

_____

_____

_____

7. What obstacles (personal or organizational) might keep you from reaching your goal?

_____

_____

_____

**104**

8. How will you and your coach know when you have reached your goal?

_____

_____

_____

## **Coaching Activity**

Employee _____

Manager _____

Monitoring start date _____

PERFORMANCE GOAL

_____

_____

| Coaching Activity Code |
| --- |
| F:  Feedback meeting |
| P:  Progress meeting |
| PS: Problem-solving meeting |
| R:  Relationship-building meeting |
| O:  Other |

| Contact Date | Coaching Activity | Next Step(s) | Next Meeting Date |
| --- | --- | --- | --- |
| | | | |
| | | | |
| | | | |
| | | | |
| | | | |
| | | | |
| | | | |
| | | | |
| | | | |
| | | | |
| | | | |
| | | | |
| | | | |
| | | | |
| | | | |
| | | | |
| | | | |
| | | | |
| | | | |
| | | | |
| | | | |

# Chapter 6

# Human Resources and Strategic Development

## The Human Resources Partnership

The Human Resources function, in our view, should be an equal partner with all other functions in the quest for organizational performance improvement. We also feel that Human Resources should be a true **strategic** partner. Effective HR strategies can mean the difference between organizational success and failure.

Before examining the potential of this partnership, it will be helpful to review the nature of the Human Resources function. The function has evolved dramatically during the past few decades. It is no longer the function that just "handles payroll" and plans the annual company picnic, but a multi-faceted function with many and varied responsibilities.

HR management, in general, is concerned about creating and maintaining formal organizational systems to ensure that human talent is obtained when required and used in the most efficient and effective way possible to meet organizational goals. There are a number of activities undertaken by the HR function. The most important of these are noted below:

- ◆ HR planning (includes HR data collection and analysis)
- ◆ Equal Employment Opportunity (EEO) compliance
- ◆ Staffing (recruiting and selection)
- ◆ HR development

- Compensation and benefits
- Employee relations
- Labor and Management relationships
- Health, safety, and security

The roles filled by HR can be categorized as administrative, operational, and strategic. The administrative role, the one that has existed historically, involves processing and record keeping. These activities include things like answering employee questions about company policy, processing benefit claims, creating and maintaining employee files, etc. The operational role typically involves identifying HR needs related to operational systems (safety training, EEO training, ensuring compliance with Federal laws, and so on) and then implementing solutions. The strategic role is concerned with the strategic use of Human Resources to gain a "competitive edge." The focus must be on the long-term implications of HR issues on organizational success. Most organizational strategic planning now includes the HR function.

As you can see, today's business environments require that HR play a significant role in organization development. This role dictates an agenda for HR. We feel that one key to your success in developmental efforts is to integrate your agenda with HR's agenda. The result will likely be a win-win situation. Now we can turn our attention to the benefits and issues related to partnering with HR.

## Organizational Strategy and Human Resources

The organizational strategic planning process is typically based on a SWOT analysis. An assessment is made of the organization's internal Strengths and Weaknesses and the Opportunities and Threats that exist externally. This data allows planners to develop broad strategies and specific plans to maximize organizational responses.

These strategies and plans must include Human Resources. Be aware of how your developmental efforts should be linked to your organization's Human Resource plans. Since every organization is concerned about the development of human resources and their consequent contribution to sustained competitive advantage, it might be helpful to review some Human Resource factors that relate to an organization's strategic success. As you can see, these factors can be linked to developmental efforts. Training, education, and experience can create or enhance them:

- Human Resources that can effectively respond to changing environments (external threats and opportunities) can play a significant role in an organization's success.

♦ Special capabilities possessed by employees can provide significant advantages. These capabilities can be enhanced by providing appropriate training and development opportunities (in addition to the employment of individuals who already possess unique knowledge and skills).

♦ HR staff members who can work effectively together, supported by the right structures and processes (in terms of HR policies and procedures), will help the organization take full advantage of its competitive strengths.

In addition to these factors, there are some other issues that must be considered when developing organizational and HR strategies:

1.  The culture of the organization (shared values and beliefs that create meaning for organization members and act as norms or rules for behavior) must be considered; otherwise, well-developed strategies can be short-circuited by a culture that is incompatible with the strategies. The perceived culture of a company also has an effect on hiring and retention—some companies are perceived as excellent places to work, while others do not enjoy a similar reputation.

2.  The life-cycle stage that an organization is in determines, in part, the Human Resource management strategies that an organization employs. There are a number of life-cycle models that are popular. Most have the same basic sequence—birth, growth, maturity, and decline. HR development activities range from basic training and development (probably purchased externally) in the so-called birth stage, internal or in-house advanced training in the growth and maturity stages, to retraining and career transition assistance in the decline stage.

## Human Resource Planning

Strategic planning must include planning for Human Resources, because business strategy ultimately determines HR strategies and activities. Developmental strategies must be created in light of the organization's goals, vision, mission, and strategies. Figure 8 illustrates the *major* variables that affect the overall HR plan for the organization. As you can see, the business strategy of the organization is implemented within the context of the organization's culture. These two variables influence the nature of Human Resource requirements (the needed number of employees who possess certain knowledge, skills, and attitudes; required training programs; policies and procedures; reward systems; and many other HR management systems). The financial resources that are available to an organization are determined by the nature of the competition, the prevailing financial environment, and the organization's current position

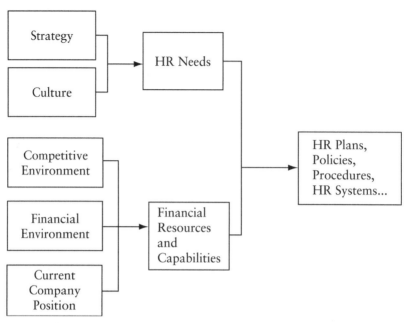

**Figure 8:** HR Plan Variables

110

(cash flow, cash reserves, credit rating, the organization's financial management capabilities, and so on). Therefore the ability of HR to meet human requirements is affected, in part, by the monies that are available—that is, the amount and availability of financial resources influence HR plans, policies, and procedures.

## Job Analysis and Design

Job information can be very valuable in terms of individual employee development needs and organizational needs (see below). The analysis of jobs can be conducted by a member of HR or, if resources permit, by an outside HR vendor. We recommend setting up an appointment with HR to discuss your potential needs.

### The Nature of Job Analysis

Job analysis involves breaking down a job into its constituent parts. The most commonly used schema in accomplishing this is job/duty/task/task element. A *job* can be thought of as a collection or set of work activities that define the total scope of work performed by an employee. If there are a number of jobs that are similar in terms of major job tasks, employees are often said to have the same job. A *duty* (sometimes called a duty area or job function) is a broad subdivision of a job that includes tasks that are somewhat related because of the nature of the tasks that are performed. *Duties* might also mean general areas of responsibility. A *task* can be defined as a discrete, organized unit of work with a definite beginning and end. A task usually starts with an action verb and includes an object of that verb (e.g., "Schedule employee vacations"). Tasks can be broken down to multiple levels, depending on the needs of the analyst. *Task elements* (sometimes called steps) provide a detailed description of how to perform a given task. Elements are sequentially connected. Figure 9 provides a graphic description of the relationship of job components.

## The Benefits of Job Analysis

A comprehensive and sound job analysis can provide important data that can serve many Human Resource planning and development needs. We have listed some of these below:

- ◆ In a broad sense, data can be used to help determine training and education needs for individuals and/or the creation of HR strategic plans.
- ◆ Data can be used in creating or modifying recruiting and selection systems.

111

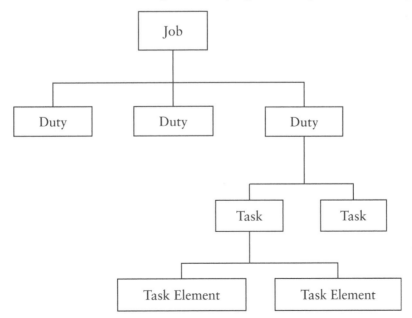

**Figure 9:** Job, Duty, Task, Task Element Relationships

- Job analysis can be used to identify work activities and behaviors that are part of a given job.
- Job information can be used to help create performance standards.
- Machines and equipment required for a given job can be identified.
- Knowledge and skills needs (both technical and non-technical) can be defined.
- Supervision requirements can be identified (both given and received).
- Other employees, functions, and entities that one interacts with in the job can be determined.

## Job Design

Job design is another area where HR might be able to contribute to meeting developmental needs. It is important to remember that individual responses to jobs can vary considerably. One employee might find that many of their job-related needs (social needs, sufficient income, challenging work, and others) are being met, while another employee who holds the same job but who has different primary or dominant needs might find the job lacking. Therefore, one person might be motivated to high performance while another might not.

The process of job design (sometimes termed job redesign) refers to organizing tasks, duties, and responsibilities (sometimes termed responsibility areas) into a productive unit of work. The design of jobs is gaining more attention these days for a number of reasons:

- Job satisfaction can be positively or negatively affected.
- Job performance, especially in situations requiring high levels of motivation, can be affected.
- Turnover and absenteeism can be positively or negatively affected.
- Physical and mental health can be positively or negatively affected.

There are certain general characteristics of jobs that can be created by developing appropriate job designs. We have listed some of the most important characteristics below. Remember, job design is aimed at creating jobs that possess some or all of these characteristics:

- A good design allows for feedback that lets an employee know how they are doing.
- A good or desirable job is usually perceived as being meaningful.
- An effectively designed job should be perceived as contributing to organizational success.

- ◆ Job design should help the job performer feel that their skills, knowledge, and abilities are being fully utilized.
- ◆ Job design should usually allow for a relatively high degree of autonomy—employees should feel that they are responsible for outcomes.
- ◆ Jobs should be viewed as avenues for personal growth.

You can work with HR to rearrange tasks, duties, and responsibilities and to redesign tasks, redefine duties, and redefine responsibilities to create "good" jobs that employees want to hold and that will contribute to personal and organizational development. There are a number of design strategies that use these activities to improve jobs. These are described in the next few sections.

## Job Rotation

When a job or certain job tasks are no longer deemed challenging by an employee or there are developmental needs and organizational needs that can be met by job rotation (sometimes called cross-training), job rotation might be a good idea. In job rotation, an employee is moved to a different job for a specified period of time—a week, a month, a year, two days per week, one day per month, and so on, depending on organization needs and capabilities. Cheraskin and Campion (1996) reported study results that help describe what an effective job rotation program looks like. Some of these are summarized below.

1. All employees have equal access to the program, regardless of demography or organizational level.
2. Employees understand rotation's role in their developmental plans.
3. Job rotation is used to develop skills and experience.
4. Employees are clear on what skills they will be acquiring or enhancing.

To aid you in deciding whether to consider the job rotation strategy as one of your developmental activities, look over this list of advantages and disadvantages and additional considerations.

On the plus side:
- ◆ Job rotation can reduce boredom.
- ◆ It can increase motivation by providing more and diverse job tasks for employees.
- ◆ Employees will likely acquire more skills and knowledge that can provide better flexibility to the organization in terms of replacing workers,

scheduling work, and being able to better adjust to changing work environments.

- Employees can gain a better overall understanding of the company's goals.
- Employees can build their networks.
- Employees can improve their problem-solving and decision-making skills.
- Employees can get a feel for what a different job requires.

On the negative side:

- Training (or re-training) costs will increase.
- There will be a temporary drop-off in productivity as the employee learns the new job.
- Rotation might cause work team disruptions.
- The supervisor or manager of an area might have to devote additional time to training the new employee or answering questions.
- High-level or experienced performers in an area might have to devote additional time to training the new employee or answering questions.
- Rotation can foster a short-term perspective in terms of problems and their solutions.

## Additional Considerations

There are some additional considerations and procedural issues to consider when you are attempting to decide if job rotation will be helpful in developmental terms. These are discussed below:

1.  Ask yourself these questions: Is rotation going to be helpful in terms of an employee's growth and development? Are the new job tasks that they will be asked to complete a stretch, or just "more of the same"?

    Very similar job tasks might not do much for development if they are not challenging.

2.  Ask yourself these questions: Are there too many new tasks that an employee must learn? Will employees be provided with enough time and training to learn new job tasks? Will they be learning the right tasks—those that will satisfy individual and organizational development needs?

3.  Spend some time with HR staff members and familiarize yourself with the areas that will be involved in rotation. Everyone involved should understand the benefits and potential costs that will be accrued and incurred. Results are likely to be better if everyone "buys in" conceptually and budgetarily.

4. Create a rotation schedule that everyone can live with. A schedule should consider changes in demand, changes in staffing, changes in budget, and changes in processes.

HR can probably help establish parameters, set up scheduling systems, make the appropriate organizational connections, help identify organizational needs, coordinate the effort, and monitor the process. Once again, before you meet with the HR department, arm yourself with a rationale for rotation.

## Job Enlargement

This is a term you sometimes hear used by HR practitioners. It is a strategy that involves expanding jobs *horizontally*—that is, increasing the number of job tasks that an individual performs. The idea is to increase job diversity. For example, when an employee completes their assigned tasks very rapidly and becomes bored, adding tasks to their job might help (if employees don't end up feeling that they are being "dumped on"). Job enlargement is not particularly effective in terms of helping employees develop, however.

## Job Enrichment

Job enrichment is a popular design strategy. It involves the *vertical* expansion of jobs. You might think of it as increasing the depth of a job. Some of the actions that can be taken to enrich a job are noted below:

- Employees are charged with doing the whole job, rather than just a piece of it.
- Performance feedback (either positive or negative) is provided on a regular basis to allow the employee to make "course corrections."
- External controls (direction provided by a superior) are decreased, while internal controls (personal responsibility) are increased.
- Increased autonomy is seen as an essential job component.
- Assignments are expanded so that new and different tasks can be learned.

## Reengineering

Another strategy that you should be aware of involves rethinking and redesigning the work itself to improve cost, service, and speed. The focus of reengineering is not the redesign of the organization's structure and the redesign of some processes, but how work flows and how jobs need to change to improve *all* of the processes associated with work. Reengineering typically involves widespread, dramatic change that focuses the organization's efforts totally on customer needs—*every* design change is made with the customer in mind. These changes might include widespread training (both technical and non-technical), redesign of the organization's processes, the creation of team-based structures, extensive cross-training, and pushing down decision-making throughout the organization. As you might guess, reengineering will result in many jobs changing because the very nature of the organization is changed. If your company decides to pursue reengineering, you will have to rethink your developmental strategies.

## Team-Based Job Designs

As you probably are aware, team-based designs to accomplish work are becoming more popular at many companies. There is a great deal of current research and experimentation with team designs that are aimed at assessing group performance versus individual performance. Space doesn't permit us to elaborate a great deal, but a plethora of information is available that you might find useful if you are considering team-based structures at your company. There are many types or categories of teams (self-directed, cross-functional, project, etc.) and many possible team configurations. Hundreds of new vendors have entered the team development arena in the past few years, making it easy to locate resources related to the use of team-based designs and the development of teams. In terms of the design of jobs and the functionality of teams, there are some design factors and considerations worth noting:

- Groups seem to be more successful in completing group job tasks when members are required to employ diverse, high-level skills (based on challenging but reachable goals and stimulating job tasks).

- Team outcomes are improved when team members view their work as having a significant impact on organization members and the organization itself.

- Task completion is enhanced when the work is viewed as a "gestalt"—having a definite beginning and end. Being able to complete a whole job or task is important.

- Team members tend to be more motivated and satisfied with the work when they are given a substantial amount of autonomy.

- When work on the task provides timely, accurate feedback on how the group is performing, the group tends to perform better.

- In order for teams to maximize their success, they should possess task-relevant skills.
- Team members should possess interpersonal skills as well as task skills that will allow them to continually assess and improve their team's internal processes and group dynamics, which largely determine team functionality.
- Team member skills and knowledge should be complementary, which will enhance synergy.

Keep in mind that if your company does employ teams, their work (and jobs) can be designed to contribute to individual development and organization development in a calculated fashion—you can integrate individual developmental goals into team developmental goals and kill two proverbial birds with the same stone.

## Task Forces and Other Teams

Assigning employees to important teams (task forces, special project teams, influential committees, strategic planning teams, and others) can provide employees with a better grasp of organizational realities. They might be able to better understand the personalities of key figures, important issues or concerns facing the organization, how organizational processes are interrelated and interdependent, and how processes *really* work.

## Succession Planning and Replacement Planning

Developing existing talent can provide a means of improving organizational performance without expending the resources necessary to bring new employees into the organization. Skills training, management development, and promotion from within can enhance organizational continuity, save limited resources, and improve morale. Replacement planning is concerned about immediate needs and a point-in-time assessment of the availability of key backups who can step in and contribute quickly. Succession planning is more concerned with long-range needs and the *development* of talent to meet those needs. Some key points related to establishing a succession plan are noted below:

- Any plan that is created must be tailored specifically to the organization— every organization's requirements are different.
- As with most initiatives, there must be top management support.
- The program should be driven by top management—not HR.
- As we know, each employee must take ownership of the process (that is, his or her own development).

- ◆ The program should be aligned with a desired or ideal culture (what the company wants to "look like" in terms of shared values and beliefs).

- ◆ Employee progress and selection should be linked to a multi-rater assessment to increase program validity.

- ◆ The program should be controlled and monitored by HR.

We recommend the creation of replacement charts to support the developmental process. Replacement charts define both needs and opportunities. The career paths that are designated by many companies represent *potential* career moves (laterals and verticals inside departments and outside departments, across departments, across divisions, and so on). Each potential path contains information regarding, at a minimum, an existing job (including its nature and relationship to other jobs), the length and type of experience required, and required knowledge and skills. The purpose of replacement charts is to help ensure that the right people are available at the right time and possess the right capabilities. Replacement charts can support the developmental process by specifying the nature of each employee's developmental needs in terms of potential promotions or transfers. Once again, succession plans are more narrow in scope and are aimed at identifying people who can or will assume positions in the future and who will be purposefully cultivated for specific jobs/roles.

# Chapter 7

## Educational Activities and Self-Development

## Training vs. Education

There are a number of different definitions for "training" and "education." We choose not to enter the semantic fray: For our purposes, *training* refers to learning activities designed to facilitate an employee's acquisition of the skills, knowledge, behaviors, and attitudes required for the performance of *specific* job tasks. We view *education* as learning activities designed to prepare an employee for advancement in the organization by helping them acquire the skills, knowledge, and attitudes that will prepare them to perform different jobs. To our way of thinking, training is focused on specific job requirements, while education is more general in nature and not related to a specific job or job task—educational activities provide a basis or groundwork for new learning. They serve an *enabling* function.

## Adults as Learners

In some ways, adult learners are the same as child learners. They react to positive or negative reinforcement, they internalize information by using rehearsal and practice, and they use the same cognitive mechanisms for forming concepts. But there are a number of differences that we should be aware of if we are going to enable our employees to prepare themselves for future work challenges. One issue revolves around the fact that child learners are, in many ways, a pretty homogeneous lot. For example, one can probably assume that any given group of fifth graders consists of 10-year-olds who are at about the same stage of physical and social development. On the other hand, a group of employees can range in age from 18 to 60 and be at different stages of psychosocial and physical development. Employees are likely to possess a range of capabilities when it comes to complex problem-solving (older and more experienced employees might be better problem solvers due to the larger cognitive "database" they are able to draw upon). Adults also have a diverse set of experiences that will affect how they perceive and behave in social situations (older adults are more likely to be "diplomatic" than some younger employees). As adults progress along the human developmental continuum, they also tend to become increasingly differentiated from one another. A group of 42-year-olds will be less like each other than a group of 21-year-olds. Therefore, educational facilitators must be aware of the potential diversity that exists in any group of adult learners, and should adjust their programs accordingly.

## Self-Directed Learners

Central to the concept of the "learning organization" is the idea that employees must become increasingly responsible for their own learning and development. This concept is mirrored by the current stance among adult educators that adults should be responsible for their own learning—they should be "self-directed." This stance is logical, since adults are much more capable of planning and choosing their own learning experiences and deciding what learning is relevant in terms of their own developmental goals. Again, they have their own unique set of experiences that differentiates them from everyone else. We have provided an educational planning document at the end of the chapter that might be useful in helping to create educational plans.

Humanistic psychology lends credence to and supports the idea that people, for the most part, are desirous of "being all they can be" and will make educational and developmental choices that will lead them toward that goal.

Adults also tend to be more positively oriented toward learning things that will help them deal with immediate problems related to social roles (which we all assume, at different points in our lives). These include parent, friend, co-worker, boss, employee, spouse, and so on. It goes without saying that our employees are likely to have different concerns based on the stage of their lives that they are in and the various roles or functions that they have assumed. Educational programs should account for and take advantage of these differences—learning activities should allow for the sharing of experiences and viewpoints.

What Adults Learn

As noted above, adults undertake educational activities to help them deal with various life-roles. Each life-role can require or be better fulfilled by various kinds of learning. For example, the role of parent might be carried out more successfully if a parent takes a child development class. The choices made by adults range all over the board—from learning the Microsoft Office software package to sculpture. We thought it would be helpful if you had a sense of the kinds of learning activities your employees might be seeking out. Data collected by the National Center for Education Statistics shows what adults are interested in.

**General Education**
- ◆ Adult Basic Education
- ◆ Citizenship Training
- ◆ High School and College Credit

**Occupational Training**
- ◆ Technical/Vocational
- ◆ Managerial
- ◆ Professional

**Community Issues**
- ◆ Civic and Public Affairs
- ◆ Religion
- ◆ Safety

**Personal/Family Living**
- ◆ Home and Family Life
- ◆ Personal Improvement

**Social Life and Recreation**
- ◆ Hobbies and Handicrafts
- ◆ Sports and Recreation

These represent broad categories or types of educational activities. As you might guess, the highest percentages of attendance are in the General Education and Occupational Training areas—learning that is likely to contribute to success in life and in society.

## Methods

The methods adult learners use to learn a subject or acquire a skill vary considerably—much more so than the methods used by child learners. The main methods used are listed below:

- ◆ Lectures/classes
- ◆ OJT (on-the-job training)
- ◆ Conferences, institutes, and workshops
- ◆ Individual lessons
- ◆ Discussion groups
- ◆ Self-study
- ◆ Correspondence
- ◆ All electronic methods

People in general still favor classroom-based learning, and companies still favor unstructured on-the-job training (OJT) by a considerable margin, but electronic learning is gaining. Conferences and workshops are also retaining their popularity.

**122**

## Reasons

Adults report that they have many reasons for continuing their learning. The most important appear to be related to (as you might suspect) knowledge goals and personal goals. We have noted some of these below:

**Knowledge Goals:**

- ◆ Become better informed about...
- ◆ Satisfy curiosity about...
- ◆ Better understand...

**Personal Goals:**

- ◆ Advance in current job
- ◆ Get certificate or license
- ◆ Get a new job
- ◆ Attain degree
- ◆ Become more knowledgeable about the industry one works in

## Educational Opportunities

### Online Learning

There are increasing numbers of educational opportunities available via the Web. Online learning includes distance learning, virtual classrooms, simulation-based learning, learning portals, and Web-based training. Learners can often control the content, control learning speed, collaborate with other learners, and control when they learn and when they practice. It is now possible to complete a bewildering array of courses online. Students can obtain certificates and "traditional" academic degrees up to and including doctoral degrees from accredited institutions. They can complete courses on almost any conceivable subject. Some of the most important advantages related to using the Web for education are noted below:

- It is accessible at any time and any place.
- Educational programs can be accessed by a geographically dispersed population.
- Learners can be linked to other employees, experts, and related content.
- Educational programs are numerous and varied.
- Learners can proceed at their own pace.
- Access to programs and courses can be faster than traditional learning.

Almost every institution of higher learning provides Web-based learning opportunities. Most can be accessed through the institution's Web site. In addition, professional organizations and vendors offer many and varied educational programs. Your own company might also have chosen to provide Web learning opportunities. Table 3 provides a list of Web addresses that might be helpful in locating and selecting educational opportunities available online.

Table 3: Internet Education-Related Resources

| Site Description | Web Address |
| --- | --- |
| Portal to knowledge management resources | www.km.com |
| Tools for creating Web learning | www.avilar.com |
| Site with a number of links to assessment tools and tests | www.2h.com |
| Site provides information on degree programs and online courses | www.edupoint.com |
| Articles and links to learning Web sites | www.brint.com |
| Career and self-development site targeted at minorities | www.imdiversity.com |
| Corporate university site | www.corpu.com |
| Learning portal | www.knowledgeplanet.com |

## Blended Learning and Learning Portals

There are some limitations to online learning that you should be aware of when you or your employees are considering educational activities. Technological issues (e.g., insufficient bandwidth, lack of ready access to a high-speed Web connection) and the preference of many employees for face-to-face instruction might indicate the need for blended learning—a hybrid approach that many companies and educational institutions are employing. Blended learning uses some combination of online, face-to-face, and, at times, other information distribution mechanisms (videos and DVD-based multimedia presentations). A blended learning approach might be more suitable for you or your employees, depending on your circumstances (given technological limitations and individual preferences). Any potential educational provider will be happy to share their approach.

Learning portals are Web sites that are used to provide access to courses, services, and links to online learning communities (see Table 3). They are a good way to locate technical and non-technical course offerings.

## Community-Based Agencies

There are a number of different types of community-based agencies that offer opportunities for education. These include many shapes and sizes of nonprofit locally or regionally oriented adult schools. Some of these exist because the local educational systems (public schools and institutions of higher education) are unwilling or unable to provide services. They are relatively few in number across the country, but they might provide an alternative education source, depending on where you are situated geographically. Included in this category are the "free" universities, learning exchanges, residential centers (nonprofit and not affiliated with labor unions, governmental agencies, universities, or colleges), and organizations that sponsor literacy initiatives.

## Proprietary Schools

These schools are privately owned profit-making schools. They include business schools, correspondence schools, and technical schools. A few are run by large companies that often provide the same or similar education externally as they do for their own employees internally. Some operate simply for profit. Some are oriented to the needs of recent high school graduates, while others serve the adult market.

**125**

## Public Schools

Many public school systems maintain evening programs that offer a wide range of topics (usually remedial/vocational and general-interest). The extent and type of offerings depend on funding (some are state-funded, while others rely primarily on federal government funds) and competition from other providers.

## Community Colleges

There are a plethora of community colleges across the country that offer two-year associate degrees, various certifications, and many non-credit options. As the name implies, they are usually charged with providing education and training services to their local community. Their range of offerings is quite broad, offering some product to almost every constituent group. Many have satellite campuses or offer programs at various sites within their service area (businesses, churches, prisons, libraries, etc.). Their delivery modes also vary considerably— classroom-based courses, seminars, video conferences, computer-based courses, Web-based e-learning opportunities, and so on.

Some of the larger schools offer almost everything to everyone. The non-credit offerings are usually provided under the auspices of a "continuing education" division. Many two-year schools are establishing agreements with four-year institutions that allow students to complete part of a bachelor's degree program before moving on to a four-year school. A number of two-year schools also maintain business and industry functions, providing public workshops/seminars or custom-designed education programs that might be of interest to you or your employees. All in all, community colleges are good sources.

## Four-Year Colleges and Universities

There are many colleges and universities sprinkling our landscape with offerings that include bachelor's, master's, and doctoral degrees. Many also offer general continuing education non-credit opportunities and support business and industry functions. Some are privately owned, while others are publicly controlled. Many offer evening, weekend, and online opportunities. Many universities also offer continuing education opportunities for professionals for general development and certification or certification renewal.

## Professional Associations

Many professional associations offer non-credit educational opportunities for their members. Some are free, some are low cost. Many associations also offer certification programs. To locate opportunities, you can visit school or association Web sites, refer to the local Yellow Pages, or contact your Human Resources department (they often maintain directories of local educational opportunities). You might also investigate the availability of tuition reimbursement.

## Training Other Employees

In our view, one of the most effective ways for employees to learn specific content is to train other employees. One caution here: It is important that employees learn how to design and deliver education and training. This strategy, of course, involves the training of employees to be effective instructors. There are many train-the-trainer programs available, some offered internally and some externally. We would highly recommend that if you are considering this approach, you investigate helping your employees acquire the skill and knowledge necessary to become effective instructors.

The educational planning document should be helpful.

## An Educational Planning Form

Employee _____    Date _____

Career Goals (long- and short-term)
Long-Term (one year or more in the future)

_____

_____

_____

_____

_____

Short-Term (this coming year)

_____

_____

_____

_____

Educational goals that will contribute to achievement of my career goals (complete degree, obtain certificate, improve my knowledge of…, acquire skill in …)

_____

_____

_____

_____

_____

_____ I have investigated all potential education providers

_____ I have met with Human Resources

# Chapter 8

# Environmental Management

## The Developmental Environment

Developmental activities take place within environments. Every environment includes forces that affect the system of which that environment is a part. In this chapter, our system of interest will be the employee who is taking part in developmental activities. In the preceding chapters, we have discussed how managers can facilitate various development efforts (coaching, mentoring, career planning, and the like). Those facilitation responsibilities should also include helping employees deal more effectively with their environments by helping them better manage stress. We have already examined facilitation activities (helping the employee network, identify potential resources, eliminate or minimize roadblocks to goal achievement, etc.). Many of these activities serve to minimize or eliminate stressors experienced by the employee. You might logically expect developmental activities to create stress, since they are often carried out in addition to "regular" duties. Lack of time often becomes an issue; this chapter addresses the management of stress in general and the management of time.

## The Nature of Stress

Stress has been defined as having three major dimensions:

Stress involves (1) **environmental demands** (called stressors), and these stressors produce (2) an **adaptive response** that is influenced by (3) **individual differences**.

The adaptive response is the well-known fight-or-flight response—we either stand and fight, or we run away. Our bodies biochemically and physiologically prepare to do either when we are faced with stressors. This response works very well when we can stand and fight or run (as our ancestors did when faced with a large cave bear). The problem is, of course, that sometimes we can neither fight nor run away from our "cave bears" (who shall remain nameless). There are also stressors like role ambiguity, interpersonal conflict, financial responsibilities, and noise pollution. Our bodies still react the same way as those of our ancestors (adrenaline flow is increased, blood leaves our extremities, some of our hormones go wild, etc.). Repeated biological changes like these take a toll over time—heart attacks, high blood pressure, headaches, strokes, insomnia, etc. The list of illnesses that might be related to or induced by stress is quite extensive.

There is positive stress and there is negative stress. Positive stress (to a degree) contributes to successful performance. In fact, we probably *need* some stress in our lives (deadlines, work goals, career goals, etc.). Positive stress keeps us focused and helps us concentrate—in fact, there are probably people you know who do some of their best work under pressure. The problem comes, of course, when we can no longer "gear down" (blood pressure stays up, stress hormone levels drop less slowly). We then become prime candidates for illness.

## Stress and Performance

There is really no question that high levels of stress affect performance negatively in certain circumstances. There is, however, some question as to the nature of the relationship. The accepted relationship (shown in Figure 10) has always been represented by an inverted "U," with performance increasing to a point, then dropping off as stress levels increase. Some studies have suggested that performance consistently declines as stress increases. Whatever the relationship, too much stress isn't good. One set of factors that affects the relative impact of different stressors is that of individual differences.

### Individual Differences

Employees often do not experience the same stressors in the same way. There are often differences in perception that serve to moderate the effect. If a given stressor is *perceived* as threatening, an employee will tend to experience more negative outcomes. Stressors are also less likely to affect employees who have a strong support network or who employ coping strategies (more on both of these later in the chapter). The type of job an employee performs is another potential

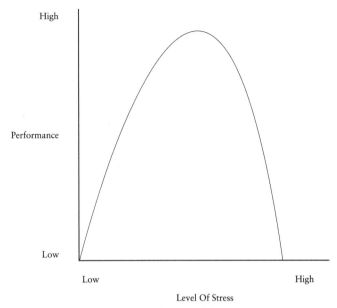

**Figure 10:** The Stress-Performance Relationship

131

moderator. Some studies have suggested that hourly employees are more at risk for stress-related illness than salaried employees.

## Types of Job Stressors

Job stressors can be categorized by:

- ◆ Stressors related to the physical environment
- ◆ Stressors related to the tasks people must perform
- ◆ Stressors related to interpersonal interactions

We have listed some examples of each of these below:

The Physical Environment

- ◆ Lighting
- ◆ Floor coverings
- ◆ Windows

- Decorations
- Furniture
- Telephones
- Music
- Voices
- Temperature
- Lack of space
- Having to share space
- Inability to personalize space
- Having to share equipment

## The Task

- Lack of equipment
- Lack of training
- Outdated equipment
- Inaccurate or poorly written procedures
- Lack of recognition
- Rewards not tied to performance
- Lack of information
- Unreasonable deadlines
- Confusion about work standards
- Too small or too great a workload
- Lack of challenging work
- Rapidly changing technologies
- Conflicting direction

## Interpersonal Relationships

- Conflict with supervisor
- Dissatisfied customers
- Problems with vendor relationships
- Competition with peers

- Being taken advantage of
- Unfairly criticized by supervisor
- No one to socialize with
- No one to share problems with
- No one to get advice from
- Unable to satisfy customers
- Poor relationships with peers
- Being forced to join an inappropriate team

You can begin the process of helping your employees deal with work stressors by having them identify their own particular sources of stress on the worksheet provided below and continued on the next page. Once these sources are identified, you and the employee can begin to take steps to eliminate them or minimize them. We have also provided an action-planning document at the end of the chapter to help you with your stress reduction planning (to be filled out after you have completed the chapter).

## Job Stressors Worksheet

In the space provided below, list job stressors for each of the categories noted. If you can, provide a rationale for why you feel the items listed are a source of stress for you.

| Job Stressors | Why this affects me |
|---|---|
| *The Physical Environment* | |
| 1. | _____ |
| 2. | _____ |
| 3. | _____ |
| 4. | _____ |
| | _____ |
| | _____ |
| | _____ |

| Job Stressors | Why this affects me |
|---|---|
| *The Task* | |
| 1. | _____ |
| 2. | _____ |
| 3. | _____ |
| 4. | _____ |
| | _____ |
| | _____ |
| | _____ |
| *Interpersonal Relationships* | |
| 1. | _____ |
| 2. | _____ |
| 3. | _____ |
| 4. | _____ |
| | _____ |
| | _____ |
| | _____ |

## Stressful Life Events

Some stressors that can affect workplace performance are experienced outside the workplace. It is important to be aware that stressful life events can affect workplace performance both directly and indirectly. We have listed some typical life events below that can affect performance and also increase an employee's statistical risk of illness:

- ◆ Divorce/Dissolution
- ◆ Death of a spouse
- ◆ Marital separation

- Death of a close family member
- Pregnancy
- Change in the health of a family member
- Death of a close friend
- Significant change in financial status
- Assuming a large mortgage
- Addition of a new family member (child or parent)

If an employee has experienced a number of stressful life events within the last year or two, their risk for illness (both physical and mental) goes up.

## Burnout

The term *burnout* has found its way into the popular press—most of us have probably used the term personally. We have used it because most of us know someone whom we believe is experiencing it. Burnout is a condition characterized by fatigue, negative attitudes, and feelings of frustration and helplessness. It is induced by stress or stress overload. It also occurs incrementally, over time. The effects of stress in burnout are cumulative, with burnout ultimately taking place when symptoms become so severe that the employee either cannot perform or simply gives up trying to perform. Burnout is often associated with high-pressure working conditions, unrealistic goals or expectations, and a lack of positive feedback or rewards.

The most obvious and effective way of dealing with burnout is to remove stressors. Some of the actions you might consider are noted below:

- Work with HR to develop realistic job previews that provide employees with a real sense of what their job will be like.
- Provide extra help at peak demand times.
- Provide increased freedom for decision making.
- Work with HR to try to provide extra time off (paid leave, compensatory time) for rest or personal development.
- Add or eliminate job responsibilities.
- Work with HR to explore the possibility for the employee to transfer to a new job or of redesigning the employee's current job.
- Increase rewards and recognition.
- Provide valid feedback on job performance.
- Increase the level of communication with the employee.

## Helping Your Employees Manage Their Stress

Now that we have examined the nature of stress and looked at some actions that might be taken to eliminate or minimize stressors, we can turn our attention to some generally accepted strategies for *managing* stress. One of the most important elements of a stress management strategy is the development of support systems.

## Support Systems

A support system is a network of resources—activities, beliefs, people, and things—that employees can draw on when times get tough. A support system can help employees resolve problems, move toward goals, provide emotional support, provide information necessary for day-to-day success, provide various types of resources, and serve as a source of social interaction. A good support system can provide employees with perspective and encouragement when they have doubts about their competence, become fearful of trying new things, or have lapsed into unproductive behavioral patterns. When employees begin to assess the people who can act as members of our support system, they should look for people who:

- ◆ Can offer suggestions on different ways to reach goals.
- ◆ Are willing to share their contacts and expertise.
- ◆ Can serve as role models.
- ◆ Can sooth our troubled soul.
- ◆ Will tell the truth.
- ◆ Are capable of inspiration.

The people who are part of a support system should be thought of as those who might help you achieve personal and professional goals while reducing your stress: parents, co-workers, supervisors, spouses, and friends. Be on the lookout for people who can be added to your support system. In Figure 11, we have provided a worksheet that can help identify who your support system consists of and assess their relative value.

It is important to keep in mind that employees need enough time and support to maintain their social relationships. If the demands of the organization are too excessive, employees' support systems will diminish in terms of their potential impact, and stress-related illnesses might increase as a result.

---

### Support System Assessment

In the spaces provided below, list the people (at work or outside of work) who you regularly seek out for support in relation to your job and career.

1. _____
2. _____
3. _____
4. _____
5. _____
6. _____
7. _____
8. _____
9. _____
10. _____

What parts (at work or outside of work) of your support system are you satisfied with?

_____

_____

_____

What parts would you like to change?

_____

_____

_____

---

**Figure 11:** Support System Assessment

## Coping Strategies

Coping is a process. This process is one that can be engaged in by employees to manage internal and external demands that have reached "critical mass." There comes a point in many careers where these demands (a.k.a. stressors) exceed or put a severe strain on the capacity of an individual to maintain their effectiveness (inside and outside of work).

137

We all have perceptual filters that affect how we interpret stressors. Some are influenced by our individual personality traits and the personal resources we have at our command (like stamina and skills). Others are situational—events might be perceived as being stressors in one situation, while not being perceived as stressors in another. We also tend to categorize stressors as being potentially harmful, threatening, or challenging and potential gain-vs.-potential loss. Therefore, the coping process involves an assessment of the stressors we are faced with (mitigated by personal and situational factors) and development of coping strategies.

Some coping strategies are attempting to control the situation, escaping from it, or managing the symptoms by employing relaxation techniques or meditation. One control strategy that you might wish to share with your employees is rational problem solving.

## Rational Problem Solving

Using a rational problem-solving model helps employees maintain their objectivity when dealing with a stressful situation. When we are in a stressful situation, we sometimes lose our objectivity because of the mental, emotional, and sometimes physical effects of the stressors we are faced with. Addressing a problem in a rational, systematic fashion allows us to better maintain a realistic view of stressors and reduce or eliminate them more effectively. The model described below is one that is commonly used to solve problems of all types:

Step 1—**Define the problem.** Be sure to create an accurate statement of the problem and why it exists.

Step 2—**Identify elements of the problem** over which *you* have control.

Step 3—**Identify all possible options.**

Step 4—**Choose the best option** based on what you think will really work and make a significant difference in terms of stress reduction.

Step 5—**Create an action plan** to implement the option you have chosen. Include a timeline.

## Self-Talk

Another strategy that might be helpful to your employees is to suggest that they engage in directed, positive self-talk. Most of us fall prey to random negative thoughts. These can be self-defeating and add to our stress levels by misdirecting our energies and eating away at our self-confidence. If we continually repeat positive thoughts about our capabilities and our ability to reach personal goals, the odds increase that we will improve our focus and acquire or enhance those capabilities. If we continually envision ourselves succeeding on the job and dealing effectively with stressors, we increase the likelihood that we actually will. The self-talk strategy has been around for a long time—probably because it works. We can often become what we envision.

## Organizational Help

As we noted earlier, a number of factors that can cause stress are controlled by management. Listed below are some actions that the organization can take under consideration as a means of helping employees cope with job-related stressors.

**Selection and placement.** The organization should consider how a given employee will react to a high-stress job. Questions included in selection interviews can address how potential employees have dealt with stressful situations in the past, and how they might envision themselves dealing with future situations.

**Job redesign.** Stress levels can often be reduced if jobs have the right amount of responsibility, are more meaningful to a given employee, and allow employees more control over how they perform their own jobs.

**Goal setting.** As we have noted a number of times earlier in the book, employees generally perform better when they have challenging, reasonable, specific goals to work toward and they receive accurate, timely feedback on performance. These same factors also serve to reduce stress levels by reducing uncertainty and enhancing control.

**Performance standards.** Well-designed performance criteria can go a long way toward helping employees know what to expect and what is going to be required of them. Knowing what lies ahead can reduce uncertainty and ambiguity, and result in less-stressful work environments.

**Involvement.** Involving employees in the decision-making process as it relates to setting job performance criteria can reduce uncertainty and increase the sense of control that an employee feels.

**Communication.** Effective, honest, and continual communication about the organization can be used to shape and modify employee perceptions. And, as we know, perceptions can play a key role in the interpretation of events as potential sources of stress.

139

Relaxation Techniques

We know that stress produces a series of physiological changes when the fight-or-flight response occurs: Blood rushes inward, hormones pulse through your body, your heart pounds, you breathe more rapidly, your blood pressure rises, and your muscles tense. These are some of the reactions to stress that gradually wear down your body's defenses and can cause serious damage over time. We cannot totally avoid stress or quickly "turn off" the fight-or-flight response, but we can learn some coping strategies that will help mitigate the effects of some of these physiological changes.

*Deep breathing.* The steps to follow when deep breathing are listed below:

1. Choose a quiet place where you will not be disturbed.
2. Choose a comfortable chair and sit up straight.
3. Let your whole body go limp.
4. Lightly rest your hands on your thighs.
5. Shut your eyes and let them remain closed.
6. Start breathing gently through your nose. Concentrate on expanding your stomach with each breath.
7. Breathe evenly, without pausing, after inhaling or exhaling.
8. After you are breathing evenly, change your breathing ratio from 1:1 to 2:1, taking twice as long to exhale as you do to inhale.
9. To help free your mind from distracting thoughts, use a mantra—a monotonous meaningless sound. For example, think "ah" as you exhale and "umm" as you inhale.
10. Repeat the process for five or ten minutes.
11. Very gradually open your eyes.
12. Sit quietly for a minute or two before resuming your activities.

Most of us do not breathe properly. We tend to take shallow breaths, using only our chest muscles instead of our diaphragms. Proper breathing can reduce the effects of stress and promote better health.

*Desk exercises.* Some exercises that employees can complete at their desks are described below. More versions can be found in exercise books, but these will get you started:

♦ **The Neck Roll.** This exercise relaxes stiff neck muscles. Gently drop your head forward, trying to touch your chin to your chest. Slowly roll your head to the right while trying to touch your shoulder to your ear. Continue with a circular motion to roll your head backward, while lifting your chin as high as possible. Slowly roll your head back around to the original starting position. Reverse direction and repeat four or five times.

- **The Shoulder Roll.** This exercise relieves tension in the neck and the shoulders. Shrug your shoulders. From this shrug position, rotate both of your shoulders forward then backward, then to your original position. Reverse position (shrug your shoulders backward and then forward) and repeat the maneuver.

- **The Back Bend.** While sitting in a relaxed position, lock your hands under your knees. Keeping your feet on the floor, *gradually* try to sit up straight. Hold the position for five seconds. Relax. Repeat three to five times. This exercise will help strengthen your back.

- **The Shoulder Stretch.** Place your left elbow in the palm of your right hand. Your left hand should drop behind your right shoulder. Using your right hand, pull your elbow to the right. Repeat for the opposite shoulder.

- **The Finger Spread.** This exercise relieves tension in your hands. With your palms facing downward, spread your fingers apart as far as possible. Hold three to five seconds. Repeat.

- **The Hug.** This one is good for tension in the shoulders and upper back. Cross your arms in front of your chest. Reach around to your back while trying to touch your shoulder blades. Hold for three to five seconds. Repeat, placing the opposite arm on top.

- **The Shoulder Flex.** This one is also good for shoulders and upper back. With your right hand, reach behind your head and over your right shoulder, and try to touch your shoulder blades. Repeat for the opposite shoulder.

## Diet and Exercise

When we eat poorly—food that is high in salt or sugar, highly refined, or over-processed—our bodies have a more difficult time dealing with the chemical demands of stress. Our bodies also use up important vitamins and minerals at a faster rate when we are stressed, often leaving us feeling listless and run down. There are many sources of information related to creating a healthy diet. Check the Web, your local library, and your local bookstores. If your company has a wellness program, it might also be a source of information related to diet. A sound exercise program also helps counteract the physical effects of stress. There are, of course, many options here, so investigation might be called for. Remember: Do not undertake any exercise program without first consulting your physician.

Other Techniques and Strategies

There are a number of other stress-management techniques and strategies that you or your employees might find helpful. Some of these are described below.

*Play.* Participating in active games, dancing, playing badminton, playing cards, and so on can be very valuable when it comes to reducing the effects of stress.

*Music.* Music can have a significant effect on your mood and how you perceive potential stressors. It can induce mental and physiological changes that dramatically affect your behavior. You probably have a very good idea about what music works for you.

*Massage.* Many benefits are to be had by way of physiological massage. It increases blood flow, relaxes tense muscles, alleviates some types of pain, calms your entire body, and reduces feelings of anxiety.

*Laughter.* Increasing numbers of medical studies suggest that laughter can positively affect your immune system and your overall health. Laughing at yourself or the situation can reap health benefits. You can also benefit from watching funny movies, comedians, and so on.

*Hobbies.* Woodworking, gardening, golf, fishing, rock collecting, bird watching, watching professional football or basketball—the activities that suit your temperament can be quite helpful in relieving stress.

**142**

## Time Management

Helping your employees manage their time more effectively is a good thing. Learning to manage *your* time can also pay dividends, because the better you manage your time, the more time you will have for your employees. Management of time connotes control, and control of time can lead to increased efficiency and effectiveness. Some commonly used strategies and techniques that can help your employees (and you) control time follow.

The Time Log

A good place to start the management process is to determine how you actually spend your time. Make up a chart that divides every day of the week into 15-minute increments. At the end of each hour, stop and jot down what you did during the preceding hour. This process can be a little tedious, but by the end of the week, you will have a very good idea of how you *really* spend your time. This is important because there is often a disconnect between how you *think* you spend your time and reality.

## Goals

As we have noted in earlier chapters, having clearly defined, prioritized goals can help you decide how to distribute your time.

## Daily Plans

One of the most important activities of the day might be to sit down and create a "to do" list for the upcoming day as soon as you arrive at work in the morning or before you leave for home the night before. You can also list (and then prioritize) the tasks that were left over from the previous day's list. In 15 or 20 minutes, you can produce a list that will give you a sense of control and direction. A good idea is to list the amount of time each item on your list will realistically require. After you have listed the tasks, assign priorities. One of our favorite methods is the "A-B-C-D." Our version is described below:

"A"    Important/Critical/Must be done now

"B"    Pretty important, but not critical

"C"    Only somewhat important

"D"    Not very important, can probably wait (maybe forever)

## Interruptions and Saying "No"

If you cannot learn to say "no," you will begin to slowly lose control of your day. You must stay focused on *your* priorities. You can also lose control if you fall prey to interruptions that divert you from the task at hand. Listed below are some commonly accepted strategies for limiting interruptions and their effects:

◆ Avoid small talk (*like the plague!*).

◆ Keep glancing at your watch or clock when a visitor stops by to talk.

◆ Induce your visitor to get right to the point. Don't be afraid to ask why he or she is there.

◆ As the old saying goes, "Be ruthless with time, but gracious with people." Provide your visitor with your undivided attention. Give them something positive before they leave (for example, an answer or an alternative meeting date).

◆ Set a firm time limit: "I have 10 minutes…"

◆ Remain standing.

143

## Dealing with Desk Clutter

It seems, at times, that we are on the verge of being buried by paper—and it never seems to stop accumulating. Even with the advent of electronic communication, most of us still get deluged with mountains of paper. Here are some strategies that might help you and your employees deal with the "paper demon":

- If possible, deal with each piece of paper right away—file it, trash it, put it into the "D" drawer.
- Set aside a small amount of time (on a scheduled basis) to pare down your paper piles. Be ruthless.
- Organize your drawers. Too many drawers become dumping grounds for finished projects and items that you plan to look at (but probably never will).
- Ask yourself, "Why am I keeping this?"
- Reduce the number of items you must file and retain. Don't keep multiple copies unless it is absolutely necessary.
- Keep your desk clear of extraneous papers. You should be working only with materials that relate to the job at hand.

## Managing the Meeting Morass

Meetings can eat up huge amounts of time. They are certainly essential to effective management, but too many meetings and meetings that are not controlled do not usually lead to productive outcomes. Listed below are some strategies and thoughts that might lead to more-effective management of meetings:

- Time limits should be set in advance and adhered to.
- Every meeting should have objectives that are clearly defined and specific.
- Distribute relative information in advance—a trip to the copier can be very disruptive.
- Decide in advance who should attend and *why* they should be there. Do not invite people just to "keep them in the loop."
- If you keep minutes, rotate the duty and set a specific deadline for distribution. Set guidelines for the form of minutes to help ensure consistency.
- Create an agenda and set limits on the time allowed for each item. Assign someone or ask for a volunteer to act as "timekeeper."

- End the meeting with a summary statement and review any actions that are to be undertaken.
- Get feedback from meeting attendees on how they thought the meeting went and what might be done differently to make the meeting more productive.

## Delegation

Many of us have more work assigned than we can handle in a given day, necessitating delegation of tasks. As manager, you must delegate effectively. Some of your employees might also be in a position to delegate and develop employees below them. Listed below are some strategies and actions that might help you or your employees delegate more effectively:

- Decide what to delegate. There might be tasks that some of your people are more qualified to perform than you are, or tasks that will provide growth opportunities.
- Choose assignments that will free up some of your time while adding to the diversity of the employee's job.
- Choose assignments that will add to the general pool of useful experience.
- Allow time for initial training and guidance. It will pay off in the long run, when the employee can perform the task on his or her own.
- Maintain communication related to progress, but stand back—everyone has to make their own mistakes.
- Maintain control in a non-directive way. Control is required for effective delegation, but no one likes to feel that they are attached by a tether.
- Make sure that tasks that are to be delegated are clearly defined.
- Make sure that you provide authority along with responsibility.
- Work at trusting your reports.

Now that we have examined some elements related to management of the developmental environment, we can turn our attention to the process of Organization Development (OD). OD aims at integrating developmental efforts to synergistically improve overall organizational performance. At the risk of being a little too repetitious, developmental activities must be undertaken in light of how they will affect the overall performance of your company.

145

## Environmental Checklist and Action Plan

*To the Employee: Complete the activities noted in the checklist below. Then complete the action planning elements. This will allow you to summarize your stressors and create a multifaceted plan for managing stress more effectively.*

I have:

- ☐ Identified job stressors in my physical environment, and determined how they might affect me.
- ☐ Identified job stressors related to the job tasks I perform, and determined how they might affect me.
- ☐ Identified job stressors related to my interpersonal relationships, and determined how they might affect me.
- ☐ Identified the elements of my support system.
- ☐ Identified coping strategies that I feel will suit my needs and my personality.
- ☐ Identified and selected time-management strategies appropriate for my job.

## Plan of Action

To eliminate or manage stressors in my physical environment, I will . . .

_____

_____

_____


To eliminate or manage job task stressors, I will . . .

_____

_____

_____

To eliminate or manage interpersonal relationship stressors, I will . . .

_____

_____

_____

I will take the following steps to build my support system:

_____

_____

_____

I will learn about, practice, and implement the following coping strategies:

_____

_____

_____

I will learn about, practice, and implement the following time management strategies:

_____

_____

_____

# Chapter 9

# Organization Development

## An Overview of Organization Development

In Chapter 1, we provided a definition and a very brief overview of the field of Organization Development (OD). We take a somewhat broader view of OD practice than some writers. As we have noted a number of times, we feel that OD is the province of *all* managers of *all* functions. This being the case, a cautionary note is in order: When a company is considering undertaking an OD effort and hiring an OD consulting firm, there is sometimes a tendency to want to shift responsibility for outcomes to the OD practitioner. The OD practitioner should not be charged with solving organizational problems and making decisions that could produce long-term ramifications for the company. Instead, this person should help organization members learn to better solve their own problems. One of their primary goals should be to improve the organizational learning capabilities of the client company, because learning *how* to learn is key to organizational success in today's world. The relationship should be one of collaboration—with the practitioner and the client working *together* to solve organizational performance problems.

OD practice provides many tools aimed at improving organizational functioning, but it should not be limited to OD practitioners—the responsibility for organizational improvement ultimately lies with *all* employees. At times, the assistance of practitioners is required (and indeed, recommended), but there are many organization development activities that can and should be undertaken by functional managers and Human Resources. We have discussed many of these in Chapters 2 through 8, but we have not integrated them into the larger OD picture. We feel that many of these developmental efforts can be facilitated and produce the best possible outcomes by helping you achieve a broad understanding of what OD is and how different types of OD activities are interrelated. Our primary goal in this chapter is to help you understand OD and how OD activities are interrelated.

This chapter provides a framework for the developmental activities described in Chapters 2 through 8. As we noted in the first chapter, all of these activities (training, career planning, mentoring, etc.) can be thought of as "interventions"—activities or actions designed to improve the performance of individuals, teams, and organizations. Where does the concept of interventions come from? A closer look at the foundations of the OD field will provide us with a preliminary answer.

## Foundations and Characteristics

OD practice is based largely on knowledge developed by behavioral science research. Disciplines such as anthropology, psychology, organizational behavior, industrial psychology, organization theory, sociology, and management have all provided the basis for the development of tools used by OD practitioners. It is important to note that many OD efforts are long-term, all are planned, and most must be sustained over a reasonably long period of time to be maximally effective. In terms of characteristics, we have noted below what we believe are some of the most important:

- ◆ **OD involves planned change.** This change is deliberate in nature. The OD practitioner purposefully sets out to create mechanisms that will induce and control the type of change desired, its magnitude, and its speed (more on change later).

- ◆ **OD often involves profound change.** One of the goals of planned change is significant, long-lasting organizational improvement at some level. This usually involves an attempt to permanently alter the organization's culture (more on culture later).

- ◆ **OD can be thought of as a process that is process-oriented.** All processes consist of flows of interrelated events that together are identifiable as a discrete entity whose purpose is achievement of a goal or an objective. All processes have an identifiable beginning and end. OD processes are aimed at improving organizational, individual, and team functioning. OD is *process-oriented* because it focuses on the processes (the how) that an organization uses, rather than the content (the what). OD is most concerned about how decisions get made, how problems get solved, about group dynamics, the dynamics of power, and so on. For example, in terms of decisions, practitioner concerns will center on how to help employees become better decision makers, not on the outcomes of decisions.

- ◆ **OD is value-loaded.** Since OD is partially rooted in humanistic psychology (remember Carl Rogers from Psychology 101?) practitioners tend to carry with them values, beliefs, and assumptions that might create "perceptual biases." These biases can color perceptions about how human beings typically behave (or should behave) in organizational settings. OD practitioners tend to believe, for example, that most people prefer cooperation over conflict and favor participative management styles. They also tend to believe that most employees want to contribute to organizational success and want to "be all they can be." These biases are not a hindrance if the organization is dominated by "Theory Y" managers. If there are a number of "Theory X" managers, however, some OD strategies and accompanying interventions might not be deemed appropriate for that particular organization.

- ◆ **OD uses the diagnostic/prescription cycle.** This process is sometimes termed the "medical model" because it involves diagnosis, prescription of treatment, administration of treatment, progress monitoring, and the taking of corrective action based on results. Practitioners approach "sick" organizations the same way a medical doctor approaches a sick person.

- ◆ **OD uses a systems approach.** Systems theory (more later) suggests that if you alter one element in a system, other elements must be or will be altered. The use of systems theory as a tool allows practitioners to maximize the functioning of the total organizational system by understanding interrelationships and interdependencies within the system. Systems theory also suggests that since almost all organizational problems have multiple causes, and solutions are likely to produce multiple effects.

Planned change and profound change are areas of significant interest and importance in Organization Development. Let's take a closer look at the nature of change.

## The Nature of Change

Change is the only constant in organizational life, but we can adapt to our dynamic environments by making changes to organizational structures and processes, and by improving the capabilities of our human resources. The

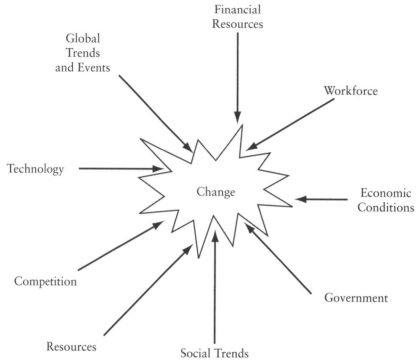

**Figure 12:** Forces for Change

primary environmental forces that can affect organizational functioning are shown in Figure 12. Examples of these forces can be found in Table 4.

Many of the forces for change noted in Figure 12 result in *unplanned change* that is too often followed by a reactive organizational response (and, sometimes rather haphazardly). As we have noted, OD is all about *planned* change—undertaking activities *specifically designed* to improve organizational functioning. Change is proactive and deliberate. Planned and unplanned changes occur in response to environmental changes (market changes, workforce changes, etc.) and are an attempt to help the organization adapt and survive.

Change is often thought of as having two different degrees of magnitude: first-order and second-order. First-order change implies no fundamental shifts in the way organization members view the world and how organizations should operate. These changes to the organization, its processes, and its Human

Table 4: Forces for Change

| Force | Examples |
|-------|----------|
| Workforce | ◆ Increased diversity<br>◆ Underskilled entrants<br>◆ Shortage of skilled professionals |
| Economic Conditions | ◆ Changes in fuel prices<br>◆ Recession<br>◆ Inflation |
| Government | ◆ New requirements<br>◆ Rezoning<br>◆ New packaging requirements |
| Social Trends | ◆ Attitudes toward smokers<br>◆ Delayed marriages<br>◆ Popularity of low-fat foods |
| Resources | ◆ Supplier price changes<br>◆ Increased costs for shipping<br>◆ Reduced availability of raw materials |
| Competition | ◆ Decreased market share<br>◆ Increased number of competitors<br>◆ Mergers and consolidations |
| Technology | ◆ Faster computers<br>◆ Better production equipment<br>◆ Cheaper computers |
| Global Trends and Events | ◆ Opening of markets in China<br>◆ Increased global competition<br>◆ Global e-commerce |
| Financial Resources | ◆ Rising interest rates<br>◆ Reduced availability of short-term loans<br>◆ Falling company credit rating |

153

Resources generally involve minor or moderate adjustments (putting a new training program in place, buying the latest piece of equipment, etc.). Second-order change, on the other hand, involves fundamental changes in the way employees think about and behave in organizational settings. It can be thought of as multilevel, multidimensional, and radical. Today, many organizations are being reinvented, re-engineered, and redesigned. Many of the old rules have changed; the nature of work itself has changed. Most early OD efforts focused on addressing first-order change, but now, faced with rapid and dramatic environmental changes, organizations are increasingly compelled to think second-order change and radically modify their companies. Many OD interventions are now designed or used to facilitate second-order change.

## Managing Change

OD is concerned with designing, implementing, and evaluating interventions that address concerns related to change. These interventions serve to help organizations manage change more effectively. To more effectively manage change, it is important to understand why people behave as they do when faced with changes to their world. If we understand the "why" of behavior, we can choose the most appropriate OD interventions.

## The Stages of Change

There are a number of "stage" models that describe what people go through as they adapt to change. One of the most commonly used models is described below:

**Stage 1—Denial.** Employees spend a good deal of time assuring one another that nothing is really going to change or that management couldn't let this happen. Acceptance of the reality of change can be very difficult for some employees, while others might display little concern.

**Stage 2—Resistance.** Employees begin to experience self-doubt, anger, depression, frustration, fear, and uncertainty. Productivity usually drops off, people start reworking their résumés, "grumbling" is rampant, and sabotage might even rear its ugly head.

**Stage 3—Exploration.** Employees have generally accepted that things are going to change. This stage is usually characterized by a lack of focus, as people try to figure out how to deal with the "new world."

**Stage 4—Commitment.** Employees have accepted that they might have to learn new interpersonal interaction patterns. Roles and expectations have been re-negotiated. Focus increases.

## Why People Resist Change

Resistance to change is largely emotional. Employees change their behaviors in response to changes in their emotions, which in turn are based on real or imagined threats to the status-quo. Some of the most common reasons for resistance are noted below:

- **Fear of failure.** Employees feel that their current capabilities will be inadequate in the new world. Self-doubt is insidious: It can lead to a lack of self-confidence and a consequent drop-off in job performance.

- **Loss of status.** Managers who lose power in a restructuring or downsizing action often perceive themselves as losing organizational power and its related status.

- **Loss of job security.** Organizational redesign often results in the redesign of jobs. Some employees feel that they will not be able to meet the requirements of a newly created job and might be viewed as "expendable."

- **Habit.** We are creatures of habit. Any change that upsets our established routines is bound to be somewhat disconcerting.

- **Fear of the unknown.** Change usually replaces the known with uncertainty and ambiguity, until employees understand what the new reality will look like.

- **Economic factors.** Some employees will be afraid that new structures, job redesign, etc., will result in a lowering of their income.

- **Threats to expertise.** Changes in organizational interaction patterns can result in wider access to information by more employees, threatening specialized workers (a good example would be access to mainframe data that was once controlled by the IT department).

- **Threats to resource control.** Some groups that have controlled sizable chunks of the company's resources envision that their staffs or budgets will be cut, thereby reducing their power and control.

## OD Strategies for Overcoming Resistance to Change

There are a number of strategies that have been suggested for overcoming resistance to change. Here are a few:

- **Communication.** Probably the most effective strategy for overcoming resistance to change is the communication of information. Employees are often the victims of lack of information or misinformation (often acquired through "the grapevine"). Communication is also critical when managing

155

the change process. People will be much more accepting if they have the facts at their disposal and don't feel that they are mistrusted and being left out in the dark. The reasons for change, the outcomes that might be likely, and the events that are occurring should be shared as often as possible, using as many channels as possible (memos, e-mail, team meetings, focus groups, and so on). It is almost impossible to over-communicate.

◆ **Participation.** With goal setting, it is difficult for any employee to resist getting onboard if they have had a hand in setting the goal. The same holds true when employees have been brought into a decision-making process that will influence the change process.

◆ **Establishment of a support system.** Human Resources can establish or broaden counseling services, provide training in new job skills, provide relocation services, or perhaps grant a short leave of absence to allow employees to deal with issues that cannot easily be dealt with during a normal workday.

We have touched on some basic concepts related to the nature of change and strategies for overcoming resistance to change—the "why" of human behavior in change situations. Now we will turn our attention to the what, how, when, and why of choosing OD interventions best suited to managing planned change.

## Systems Thinking and OD

Systems thinking, based on open systems theory, provides a powerful conceptual tool for understanding organizational dynamics. Almost all OD practitioners use the precepts and concepts proffered by General Systems Theory (GST). These were first articulated by the biologist Ludwig von Bertalanffy in the early 1950s. Although his initial interest was biological systems, as he continued his research, he began to think on a broader scale: He looked for principles that could be applied to all systems, not just biological ones. He and a number of his colleagues worked for some years to develop a theory that would provide generalizations that could be applied to virtually *any* body of scientific work, from the study of a single cell to planet Earth. The key idea, then, is that these generalizations can be applied to *any* system. In the 1960s, GST principles began to be applied to organizations (complex systems). A system has been defined as:

> *A collection of interdependent, organized parts that work together in an environment to achieve the purpose of the whole.*

As you can see from the definition, *system* denotes interdependency, interrelatedness, and interconnectedness (organized parts working together) that can be identified and defined as a whole (a distinct entity). Figure 13 provides a graphic representation of any (and all) systems.

The characteristics of systems can be very important in OD practice. Since system elements are interrelated, interconnected, and interdependent, what is done to one element of a system affects what happens to other elements in the system. When an intervention is selected, it must be chosen with a view toward how it will affect other elements in the system. Since all systems are also subsystems of some larger system, you must also consider how changes might affect other subsystems. For example, let us suppose that we have defined our system of interest (an organizational subsystem we are going to intervene in) as Department Y, a data entry function. Department Y has inputs of various types, as all systems do. It also has work processes that use the inputs of that department. These work processes operate on the inputs to produce outputs, which in turn become the inputs for other subsystems.

If a training program for data entry operators designed to improve their speed and accuracy is successful, the output of the operators will increase. These questions should be asked before the program is put in place: What effect will increased output have on the functions that receive input from Department Y? How will input requirements to Department Y be affected? What might happen in terms of the internal dynamics of Department Y? Will other department members resent the training (and possible compensation increases) that Department Y members will receive? The big picture must be considered before an intervention is implemented.

Systems theory also allows us to define the system we are going to intervene in— the whole. We can choose to intervene in a department, a production line, a portion of a production line, a work team, a division, even the whole organization. The benefit is obvious: By defining the systems of interest, it becomes much easier to determine the likely outcomes of interventions in relation to other organizational subsystems. It is also much easier when diagnosing an organizational problem to pinpoint or isolate a problem's root cause.

GST also provides perspective. Since every system exists in its own distinctive environment, GST helps us remain aware of how environmental changes can affect the functioning of a given system.

Peter Senge in *The Fifth Discipline* (1990) summarizes the issue we face as we attempt to diagnoses organizational performance problems:

> *From an early age, we're taught to break apart problems in order to make complex tasks and subjects easier to deal with. But this creates a bigger problem . . . we lose the ability to see the consequences of our actions, and we lose a sense of connection to the larger whole.*

Environment

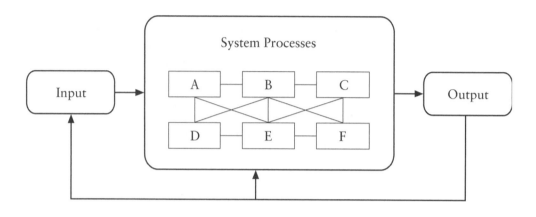

Feedback Loop

**Figure 13:** A System

## The Nature of Systems

As you can see, GST provides a tool to help in diagnosis (more on diagnosis later). Since a systems view of organizational problems is critical in terms of organization development, we felt that it would be beneficial to examine some of the characteristics common to all systems. These are described below:

1. The *elements* of a system are affected by being in the system and are changed by being taken out of it. You can never fully understand a system element unless you study it in the context of the system to which it belongs.

2. Systems have multiple *environments*. An individual employee can constitute the basic system. The employee might belong to a team that is part of a department that is part of a division, and so on. A good way to visualize multiple environments is to visualize concentric circles. Once again, the investigator defines the systems.

3. Systems have *boundaries*, but most of these boundaries are permeable—that is, they exchange information with their various environments. Outside forces cause internal changes.

4. The law of *entropy* states that all systems "run down" and collapse unless they achieve a state of "negative entropy" by creating enough outputs that can be exchanged for inputs that will keep the system running. The key

here is to modify the system in such a way (by using appropriate interventions) that it continues to produce the right type and quantity of outputs to keep the system in balance.

5.  Systems depend on *feedback* from their environments to maintain optimal performance.

6.  Systems also strive to maintain dynamic *homeostasis* (steady state). Homeostasis indicates that a system is in a state of equilibrium, or balance, that is a result of adapting to disruptive internal and external forces. Humans provide a good example: The human body strives to maintain a constant internal temperature that serves to maintain the integrity of the organism— a few degrees one way or the other and the body becomes stressed.

7.  Over time, systems tend to become *differentiated*—more complex, specialized, and elaborate. This characteristic is readily apparent as organizations grow.

8.  Another characteristic of systems is that of *equifinality*—a GST principle that states that there are multiple ways to arrive at a particular outcome or state, just as there are multiple pathways to the solution of a problem.

To summarize, open systems thinking underlies OD practice. The principles and concepts of GST provide tools that allow the practitioner to better solve organizational performance problems and aid in the developmental process.

Now that we have explored organizational change and examined the role of systems thinking in diagnosing and improving organizational performance, we can turn to the actual practice of OD.

## The OD Process

The OD process is an iterative one that involves diagnosis (assessment), taking action (interventions), re-diagnosis (reassessment), evaluation (of the interventions), and new actions (new interventions). This problem-solving process has been used as the basis for development of what is often termed the **Action Research Model.** This process model is illustrated in Figure 14. The process is described in some detail below and on the following pages.

## The Action Research Model

This model, used widely by practitioners, is based on the general OD process model. There are other models and approaches to organizational improvement, but this tool is popular because it incorporates some key features that increase

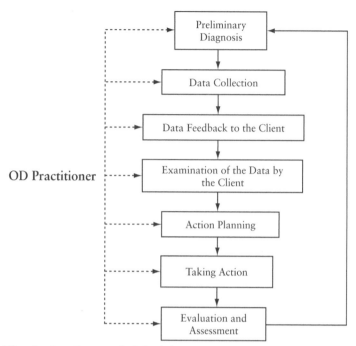

**Figure 14:** The Action Research Model

the potential effectiveness of change efforts: Organization members are required to participate, contribute ideas, and provide solid data. This type of full participation helps ensure better results and increased commitment to intervention activities. As you can see in the graphic, the OD practitioner serves as a *facilitator* throughout the entire process; the client is responsible for supplying data, making decisions, planning, implementing, and evaluating. After we have examined the Action Research Model, we will take a closer look at the steps in the OD process.

## Preliminary Diagnosis

In preliminary diagnosis, the organization attempts to gain an initial understanding of problem or opportunity areas. The current state or situation is examined in order to understand things as they really are.

## Data Collection

This step involves collection of data related to the problem or opportunity identified and defined in the preliminary diagnosis step. Data is gathered from the client group.

## Data Feedback to the Client

The data that has been collected from the client is evaluated, ordered, and presented to the client by the practitioner. An interpretation of the data might be offered to the client. The meaning and impact of the data is discussed.

## Examination of the Data by the Client

The client examines and explores the data to determine possible actions that can be taken to address the problem or opportunity. The facilitator can share his or her thoughts regarding possible options and strategies.

## Action Planning

The client, with help from the facilitator, creates an action plan to implement the initial actions (interventions that have been decided upon). The action plan would include possible roadblocks to implementation and resources (financial and human) that will be required. A program management plan or strategy is also developed.

## Taking Action

At this stage in the process, the client implements the action plan. Program management activities help ensure that the plan's goals and objectives are being met.

## Evaluation and Assessment

Based on pre-established performance criteria, the client, with help from the facilitator, evaluates the degree of success of the actions undertaken. If results are positive, the process can end (except perhaps for planned follow-up activities). If results are not positive, the process should begin again (with further data collection and the like). Goals and objectives can or should be revised.

## Diagnosis

As we see it, diagnosis is the most important part of the OD process. Diagnostic activities allow you to really "figure things out"—that is, determine the actual state of affairs. Data collected during the diagnostic phase also allows you to get a good idea of what effect different interventions will have on the organization system, its subsystems, and its processes. Data are usually collected by means of surveys, diagnostic meetings, individual and group interviews, observation, examination of organizational records, organizational performance data, and confrontation meetings. Listed below are the subsystems and processes usually targeted at one point or another during the diagnosis phase:

- **The total organization.** The entire organization and its subsystems are analyzed to get a handle on culture, organizational attitudes, climate, the functioning of operational and interpersonal processes, team dynamics, mission and vision, management styles, and so on. This analysis also includes other organizations that make up the environment of the organization being analyzed (suppliers, government, activist groups, customers, etc.).

- **Major organizational units.** Divisions, regions, and functional departments (manufacturing, accounting, etc.) are the systems of interest here. Information sought here is the same as that for the total organization. In addition, practitioners wish to determine the nature of the relationships that exist between these subsystems and the larger organizational system. It is obviously important from a management perspective to know if goals, objectives, missions, visions, and resource utilizations are in alignment with the total organization.

- **Work groups and teams.** This group includes all of the typical teams (for example, task forces, project teams, permanent teams, various cross-functional teams, and top management teams) and formal work groups. Team processes (for example, decision making, goal setting, planning) are investigated. Also examined are team dynamics, organizational attitudes, resource utilization, and so on.

- **Individual employees.** This group includes all the employees of the company. Employee attitudes toward the organization, organizational subsystems, and functional areas are typically examined. Performance is also assessed in terms of the standards employed by the company. Roles are examined. Knowledge, skills, and abilities are assessed. Career paths and career opportunities are often evaluated.

- **Organization processes.** There are many processes that can or should be examined during analysis. These include processes such as formal and informal communication, conflict management, decision making, superior-subordinate relations, problem solving, strategic planning, visioning, and technology introduction.

It is important to note that diagnosis never ends. Organizational environments are continuously changing, so the need for adaptation is continuous. OD is an ongoing quest to generate data on how the systems of interest are performing.

## OD Interventions

After the diagnosis phase is complete, action is taken to "fix" problems or take advantage of opportunities that have been identified. (There might also be alignment problems to consider). These actions are termed **interventions**. Interventions take many forms. They include team-building activities, changes to the organization's selection system, conflict management training, role clarification activities, and so on. The list of potential interventions is extensive. (We will take a closer look at intervention typologies a little later in the chapter). After selected interventions are employed (based on their likelihood of success), an evaluation is made to determine how successful they were in terms of meeting the goals of the OD strategy (overall OD plan). If required, new interventions are undertaken.

Just as teams must focus on both content and process to be maximally effective, so must OD practitioners. They must also, of course, consider subsystem inter-relationships, bring people into the process, and provide appropriate and timely feedback to the client. In other words, in order for an OD effort to be effective, it must be *managed*, just as every other organizational activity is.

## The Impact of Organizational Culture

Culture has been defined as:

> *A system of shared meaning held by members that distinguishes the organization from other organizations.*

Some writers conceptualize culture as the "social glue" that binds organization members together. This "glue" can be thought of as being made up of things like shared values, shared ideals, rituals, stories, and material symbols (often called "artifacts").

Culture can be a very positive force in terms of organization development goals—or it can be a very negative one. It is often assumed that a strong culture, one that is highly cohesive with many strongly shared values and shared commitment to goals, is a positive thing. It may be, but not if it is a change-resistant culture—one that does not value change. A weak culture that is innovative might be a better bet in terms of potential organizational performance.

It is also important to remember, from an OD perspective, that culture is sometimes not uniform across the organization. There is usually a *dominant culture* that expresses the *core values* held by a majority of organization members, especially in larger organizations. Hence, a certain number of shared core values among organization members exist, but *subcultures* with additional values that reflect unique shared experiences or common problems and situations tend to develop. These "minicultures" are typically defined by department designations and geographical location. For example, the accounting department might have a unique culture that is shared only by department members. Since OD is often concerned with changing cultures in some way, it is important to understand the nature of the culture that you are dealing with so that appropriate interventions can be chosen.

All in all, changing a culture in a really substantive way is very difficult and usually requires years of concerted effort. Most cultures are resistant to large-scale change; relatively discrete (limited scope) and incremental change is the norm in OD practice (although some programs are very broad in scope). OD efforts are generally focused on long-term, sustained change that is well-planned and integrated into the organization's subsystems. There are a few situations, though, that might provide an impetus for culture change or create an environment that can facilitate change, even though significant change will still require significant time. Some of the most important drivers of change are listed below:

- **A weak culture.** Weaker cultures tend to react easier to change than stronger ones.

- **A youthful organization.** Younger, smaller organizations are less likely to be firmly attached to value sets. Acceptance of a new direction is likely to be easier.

- **A crisis.** A crisis might present itself at any time. Major financial setbacks and unforeseen moves by a competitor tend to create a need for significant organizational change. The organization might have to reinvent itself should such an event arise.

- **A leadership shift.** New leadership might bring with it an entirely new set of key values.

Some typical actions that might be undertaken are listed below:

- The organization's reward system might be modified to support new values.

- Current subcultures might be restructured by transfers, job rotation, and perhaps even termination (as a last resort).

- New stories and rituals might be disseminated.

- Employees who identify with, support, and espouse the new values might be promoted.

- New artifacts might be introduced.

◆ The selection system might be modified to allow for the employment of individuals who hold the "correct" values.

## Intervening

OD interventions can be thought of as *sets* of structured activities that are targeted at specific individuals, groups, or processes, with the goal of performance improvement. Behind every program is an overall game plan or strategy that includes:

1. A clear statement of the goals and/or objectives of the interventions.
2. The expected and desired outcomes.
3. A clear statement of the problem or opportunity to be addressed.
4. The sequencing of the interventions.
5. The timing of the interventions.

A program is generally structured in an incremental fashion and is designed to change the current state to some future state over an extended time period. Figure 15 illustrates this process.

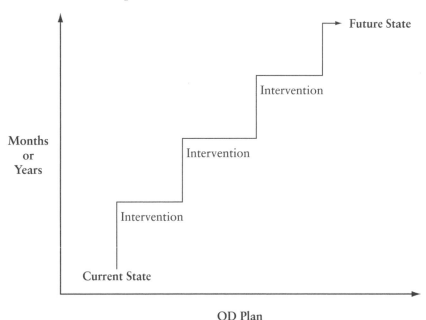

**Figure 15:** Program Process

## Intervention Design

Most interventions are designed to facilitate and promote learning and change. That being the case, many principles that apply to creating sound instructional systems also apply to the design of interventions. Some of the more important principles that apply to interventions and learning activities are listed below:

- Adults learn more readily if the content (the what) and the processes they are attempting to internalize (the how) are focused upon *real* problems that hold some personal significance—those that are *relevant* to them.

- Learning activities that are problem-centered are more effective if the employees who are affected by the problem and its solution are *included* in the problem-solving process.

- Activities should be *goal oriented*; the goal should be clearly stated, along with the path to reach the goal.

- Activities should be structured so that they include *conceptual* learning as well as *hands-on* experiences. Learners should have a chance to apply newly acquired concepts.

- All activities should be designed with the over-arching goal of helping employees *learn how to learn*. This is one of the major goals for creating a learning organization.

- Activities should be constructed so that there is a *high probability of success*—an important feature that applies to *any* goal.

- The learning *climate* should be free of risk, allowing employees to work together on problem solutions without fear of censure or ridicule.

- Activities should be *logically sequenced and timed* to conserve organizational resources and prevent duplication of effort.

- Learning is more likely to occur if employees are asked to learn what they perceive as having some impact on *their own situation*. It might be necessary to help employees understand why learning something is important to their own personal success: because personal success is, at times, based on organizational success.

- When designing interventions, it is important to understand that interventions have different results because they are based on different *causal mechanisms*. You must understand the causal mechanisms if you want to increase the likelihood of success—things like inadequate procedures, gaps, or discrepancies in knowledge and skill; interpersonal relationship issues; and cultural and structural issues must be identified and assessed.

### Intervention Outcomes

Many intervention outcomes will result in change. The list below gives you an idea of the kinds of outcomes that are possible from an OD effort:

- Improved communication
- Role clarification
- Acquisition of skills
- Acquisition of knowledge
- Increased employee participation
- Conflict resolution
- Increased interaction
- Increased/improved performance feedback

These outcomes can be achieved in multiple ways (that is, by using a number of different interventions).

### Intervention Classification

The OD intervention inventory is extensive (there are literally hundreds of different ones). A number of representative interventions are noted in Figure 6: Gap Analysis. Typologies or classification schemes can help you think about your intervention options. Some of the major groups or types are listed below in commonly used categories. (Remember that this is just one classification scheme.)

- **Team-building activities.** These include activities designed to improve the functioning of any kind of team. Different interventions are typically designed or employed to address conflict issues, group dynamics, process issues, skill and knowledge acquisition, and leadership issues.
- **Survey feedback.** Surveys are probably the most widely used diagnostic tool in OD practice. Data is collected via surveys and used to address *many* different types of organizational performance problems.
- **Training.** Training interventions are aimed at narrowing or eliminating the performance gap discussed in Chapter 3. These activities are used to help employees acquire knowledge and skills or modify their attitudes. There are *many* different types of training activities that can be employed.
- **Intergroup activities.** These interventions are used to improve the effectiveness of interdependent groups. Some work groups (this includes teams)

167

must work together to reach common goals. Intergroup activities are designed to facilitate this process.

- **Coaching activities.** These activities involve a consultant or coach working with individual employees to solve learning and performance problems. Providing valid, nonjudgmental, and timely feedback is an integral part of many of these activities. Revisit Chapter 5 for a detailed discussion of coaching activities.

- **Third-party peacemaking.** Typically conducted by a consultant, these activities are designed to help two employees resolve or manage their interpersonal conflicts when other interventions have not been effective. **A cautionary note:** If you do hire a consultant to conduct these kinds of activities, be sure you examine their credentials closely; third-party peace making requires a high skill level.

- **Career planning.** These activities are designed to help individuals examine their career goals and devise action plans to reach them. See Chapter 2 for a detailed treatment of career planning.

- **Planning and goal-setting.** These activities are designed to provide or improve skills in long- and short-term planning, problem solving, team and individual goal setting, and so on. These activities are often conducted at different levels: for the total organization, for teams and work groups, and for individual employees.

- **Diagnostic activities.** As we noted in our earlier discussion of the diagnosis process, there are a number of diagnostic activities designed to determine the true "state of the system" and the root causes of performance problems at the individual, process, and organizational levels.

## Technostructural Interventions

There are a number of interventions that seek to jointly optimize the technological and social systems that exist in all organizations—that is, to integrate people more effectively with work systems (the means by which work is accomplished). These interventions typically focus on changing tasks, processes, or organizational structures, and modifying existing technologies or introducing new technologies. We have listed some of the intervention targets for technostructural interventions below:

- The overall design of the organization
- The design of teams and work groups
- The introduction or refinement of technologies

- The physical work environment
- Communication processes
- Job design
- Quality improvement systems
- Appraisal systems

## Learning Organizations Revisited

We discussed the concept of learning organizations in Chapter 1. Proponents (we are among them) believe an organization can be at least a partial remedy for a number of problems that it experiences, such as so-called silo management, where functions are separated into little kingdoms that often vie for a limited resource pie, power, or influence. Another problem is related to an over-emphasis on internal competition that serves to limit collaboration and sharing of information. "Reactive management" or "putting out fires" (rather than proactively managing) is another. Few organizations become the learning organizations described in the literature, but we believe that becoming one is a worthy goal. Many of the goals that will help a company become a learning organization are very positive in terms of overall organization performance—improved communication, reduction of the "silo" mentality, decision making that takes place throughout the organization, leadership that is shared by all employees, employees becoming much more aware of the "big picture," and so on. Some of the more important characteristics of learning organizations are listed below:

1. There is a shared vision that everyone buys into.
2. People change their ways of thinking about what organizations should be like and how they should treat people.
3. People discard old, inefficient ways of doing things and continually search for new and better ways. Innovation is rewarded.
4. Employees continually learn and try to improve their skills and gain new knowledge in their own domains.
5. Employees take a systems view of organizations and realize that all organizational systems are interrelated and interdependent.
6. People communicate freely up, down, and across the organization.
7. The organization design is team-based. Cross-functional teams become the order of the day.

169

8. People push aside their own personal self-interest and work together to achieve the organization's goals and vision.

9. The leaders become "servant leaders" who are concerned about the success of individual employees and about creating a positive, motivating work environment.

10. A work environment is fostered that allows employees to offer the best of themselves and causes them to feel that they *are* the company and therefore have a vested interest in its long-term success.

You can also think of the items in this list as *goals*. Space does not allow for a full treatment of the learning organization, but we highly recommend that you investigate the many resources currently available that will provide you with the tools you need to transform your company into one that is continually learning and that is ever more capable of dealing with today's challenging environments. Managers are in the unique position of being able to change themselves and the work environment so that the organization's human captial can develop to potential. As we explained at the outset, organizational success is increasingly linked to team success.

**170**

## Problems Related to Developmental Efforts

A few common mistakes and problems connected to Human Resource development efforts are worth revisiting. As you do developmental planning, make sure you keep an eye on these pitfalls:

- Inadequate up-front analysis that fails to really define and delineate the organization's developmental needs
- Managerial abdication of employee development (managers are ultimately responsible for the development of their own employees)
- Relying on courses as the primary developmental tool
- Lack of planning for transfer of training
- Lack of training for developmental leaders (line managers, coaches, mentors, non-professional trainers)
- Attempting to substitute training for sound selection practice
- Trying out fad programs without adequate research into their quality

## Working with Consultants

There are a number of guidelines and issues that we feel should be considered when establishing a relationship with a consultant. Listed below are some of the most important:

- If you have a better handle on the problem than the potential consultant, don't hire them. Why waste time and money?

- Spend your time up front. Clearly define your project and your needs. You'll save time and money in the long run.

- Don't be afraid to ask for referrals. The consultant's experience level might be very important on your project. Get the best contact information that you can (past client job titles, project type, e-mail addresses, and the like).

- If a consultant agrees to give you what you want even though he or she initially suggested other options, don't hire this person. Good consultants will stick to their guns if they feel strongly that doing what you want would be a disservice to you.

- On the other hand, if a consultant is not flexible after examining all the data (assuming your position is solid) and insists on doing everything his or her way, agree to disagree, and look for another consultant.

- Depending on the nature of the project, it might be helpful for the consultant to understand your local market and industry.

- Is there a positive chemistry between you, the consultant, and your team?

- You might want to subdivide a large project into smaller ones to "try out" a consultant before signing a large contract.

- Appoint a liaison who can deal with minor problems and needs (arranging for facilities rental, equipment rental, setting up meetings with subject-matter experts, etc.). The liaison might also be responsible for dealing with minor problems faced by the consultant and for reporting back on the consultant's progress.

- Do as much of the work up front as you feel comfortable with.

- Get down on paper *all* the terms and conditions of employment, with as much detail as possible (deliverables, timelines, cost over-run responsibilities, special pricing arrangements, *who* will deliver the services, reporting arrangements, and so on). If you are using a standard consultant contract, you may wish to add an addendum if the standard contract does not cover all the bases.

## Some Final Thoughts

We believe that organization development should be a necessary and integral part of *organizational strategy*. It is becoming more apparent that without a really concerted, far-ranging development effort closely linked to the organization's vision, it will become increasingly difficult for that organization to effectively compete in the new marketplace. We hope the tools provided in this book will give you the confidence to tackle employee and organization development. OD education should be an ongoing process because of the important role it plays in the success of an organization.

We wish you the best of luck.

# Selected References

Beer, Michael & Walton, A. E. (1987). Organization change and development in *Annual Review of Psychology*, edited by Mark Rosenzweig and Lynn Porter. Palo Alto, CA: Annual Reviews Inc.: pp. 339–340.

Cheraskin, L. & Campion, M. (1996, Nov.). Study clarifies job rotation benefits. *Personnel Journal*, 31–38.

Drucker, Peter F. (2001). *The essential Drucker: the best of sixty years of Peter Drucker's essential writings on management.* New York: HarperCollins Publishers, Inc.

Gagne, R. & Medsker, K. (1996). *The conditions of learning.* Florence, KY: Wadsworth Publishing.

Kirkpatrick, D. L. (1994). *Evaluating training programs: the four levels.* San Francisco, CA: Berrett-Koehler Publishers.

Mager, R. & Pipe, P. (1970). *Analyzing performance problems.* Belmont, CA: Pitman Learning/Lake Publications.

Mills, D. Quinn. (1991). *The rebirth of the corporation.* New York: John Wiley and Sons.

## Kalamas Book

In today's rapidly changing business environment, companies can no longer rely solely upon traditional venues for gaining a competitive edge. The playing field has been leveled. Most companies have access to the same or similar technologies and can employ people with similar skill sets, leaving few with a competitive edge.

To be successful, companies must create a climate that encourages employees to continuously develop themselves, become better performers in their own areas of expertise, and acquire a sense of ownership for the organization's success (or failure).

This book provides a very *comprehensive* treatment of individual and organizational development. It also provides guidelines for managers to *set the stage*—establish work environments that are conducive to self-development.

This book will help you:

- Redesign and rethink your strategies for individual and organizational development.
- Integrate developmental strategies.
- Link Human Resource plans with corporate strategies.
- Better manage the developmental environment.
- Create a viable organization development plan.
- Give your organization a competitive edge.
- Make sound decisions about training interventions.
- Design, develop, implement, and manage coaching and mentoring systems.
- Help your employees develop career plans.

# About the Authors

**David J. Kalamas, Ph.D.,** has worked in the Organization Development (OD) field for over 20 years, serving as a manager of training and development at a number of different institutions and as an HR manager responsible for providing OD services to local business and industry. His work experience also includes a six-year period with a large financial institution, where he served as a performance consultant and trainer. Dr. David has had direct experience in almost all areas of OD practice. He currently teaches in an MBA program at a local university and consults in the field of organizational development. His published work focuses on training and development and adult education.

**Joan Berry Kalamas** is a certified Senior Professional in Human Resources (SPHR), with over 20 years of experience in the private, public, and educational sectors. She is the president and founder of Strategic Solutions, an HR consulting and continuing education provider company. Joan teaches extensively in MBA and undergraduate business programs for Ashland University and Capital University, and teaches in the Business and Industry Institute at The Ohio State University/Central Ohio Technical College.

Joan is the Central Ohio district director for the Ohio State Council of the Society for Human Resource Management. She was a member of the Board of Directors of the Human Resources Association of Central Ohio for many years, serving as president of the association in 2001. Joan holds a bachelor's degree in Education from Ashland University and a master's degree in Professional Development and Adult Education from The Ohio State University. She is a frequent presenter.